THE SANIBEL ISLAND LIGHTHOUSE

A Complete History

A history of Sanibel Island's oldest modern structure, and the land surrounding it, presented through a first-person account using fully interpreted old photographs and postcards.

by
CHARLES LEBUFF

SANIBEL BEND

Conchosis by Enid P. Donahue

Forgive me, my dear, for not writing..
  I fear a most tragical end:
My head is bent low; my footsteps are slow..
  I've come down with the Sanibel Bend.

Each morning I follow the ebb tide;
  I'm aimlessly searching the sand;
I've a crick in my neck; my elbow's a wreck
  From balancing shells on my hand.

My shoes are quite worn to a frazzle..
  I'll be glad when my holiday's done!
I've lost thirty pounds while doing the rounds..
  I'll soon fade away to a ton!

I've a curve in my neck like a heron;
  My nostrils the sea smells offend;
I stick out at the back from this vicious attack
  Of the malady, Sanibel Bend.

But ah! What a ghastly psychosis!
  For the worst of it is, so they say,
Once you've had an attack, it always comes back.
  And you come to the Island to stay.

* * * *

It isn't the miles that you walk that count;
  Nor the fish you catch and proudly mount;
Nor the shells you find of various hue;
  It's just that HERE is the place for You.

© COPR. 1953, WILFRED FUNK, INC.

DING DARLING

Sanibel Island is world-renowned for its reputation as one of the best beaches on Earth to visit if you are a seashell collector. This postcard typifies the famous "Sanibel Bend" (aka "Sanibel Stoop") that is exhibited when shellers bend over to inspect the beach surface while move hesitantly along the wrack line in hopes of finding a rarity like the Junonia or lion's paw. Note the artwork was rendered by winter resident J. N. "Ding" Darling. *From the author's collection*

Copyright © 2017 by Charles LeBuff

All rights reserved. This book may not be reproduced or transmitted in any form or by any other means—graphic, electronic, or mechanical, including photocopying, burning, recording, or any information storage or retrieval system—without written permission from the author.

PUBLISHING

14040-101 Eagle Ridge Lakes Drive
Fort Myers, Florida 33912

Visit us at:
http://www.amber-publishing.com

ISBN 10: 0-9625013-3-6
ISBN 13: 978-0-9625013-3-3

The Cover: The illustration used on the cover is a modification of the 1955 postcard used on page eight. For classic automobile buffs, and people interested in knowing something about the vehicles in the foreground: The car to the left is a 1948 Chevrolet Fleetline and that on the right is a 1953 Nash Ambassador. *Islander Trading Post*

Charles LeBuff

OPPOSITE PAGE—This was the business end of the Sanibel light tower in 1966. The lower gallery (railing and walkway) surrounds the windowless watch room. A double-door leads outside and an exterior ladder provides access to the smaller upper gallery that encircles the lantern room. Look carefully, notice the black object positioned at the center of the rail (just above the lens). This is the "sun valve" that once turned the lighting system on and off. The lens pictured is the 500-millimeter optic that was the third to be used in the lighthouse. On the left and outside of the lantern room one of the handholds is clearly visible. One of these is bolted to each of the 10 metal mullions that hold the glass in place. These grips allowed a light keeper to hold on firmly whenever they periodically and bravely cleaned the exterior of the heavy plate glass storm panes. When this photo was taken real glass still enclosed the lantern room. A few years after electrification (1962) the plate glass storm panes were replaced with acrylic. Over time this darkened, became partially opaque; etched by long-term interaction of sea salt-laden mist. When the light tower was completely rehabilitated in 2013 real glass again was installed to wall the lantern. *Charles LeBuff*

In this photo from 1960 the second Third Order Fresnel lens is in place. It served the Sanibel Lighthouse from 1923 to 1962. The sun valve is clamped to the upper railing on the eastern side of the tower. *Charles LeBuff*

INTRODUCTION

THIS BOOK IS AN OUTGROWTH OF MY INTENSE PERSONAL interest in the history and operation of the Sanibel Island Light Station. This historic facility is located in Lee County, on the coast of Southwest Florida. The light-supporting tower and buildings at this station were the first of three lighthouse complexes, excluding range lights, to be built in Southwest Florida. It is the most prominent of the remaining two which continue to stand as coastal sentinels between the still functional older lighthouses on Loggerhead Key (built in 1858) in the Dry Tortugas, and the original structure at Egmont Key (also built in 1858) at the entrance to Tampa Bay.

Lighthouses in the United States are often referred to as "America's castles," and like many European castles, many of our lighthouses have fallen into serious disrepair. Most are no longer operational; they are victims of obsolescence because of a growing body of navigational technology. Men and women no longer serve as resident lighthouse keepers. Gone are those respected pillars of lonely and isolated communities.

The Sanibel Island lighthouse is today classified as unattended and automated, but it remains a functioning aid to navigation. My life has been inextricably associated with this antique structure since 1958, but my personal recollections and interactions with this old beacon now span over 65 years. In this book I weave a narrative account about major events connected to the history of Sanibel Island.

The Sanibel Island Light Station is the key element from which the island's modern history sprang. I hope to take you on a trip back in time as I present the story of Sanibel's lighthouse in an educational and interesting format. I have tried to keep in mind that it is difficult to write a spellbinding account about all the dull mechanics of inanimate objects. Fortunately, there are human elements associated with lighthouses, too. I hope to hold your attention by interlacing interesting facts with photographs from earlier times. It is my purpose that after you finish reading this account and wandering through the illustrations you will have learned something—and that you enjoyed the experience.

In the 1990s I represented the Sanibel Lighthouse as a board member of the Florida Lighthouse Association. This rapidly growing organization is a force in lighthouse protection and their educational interpretation. The not-for-profit organization's quarterly meetings are held at various lighthouses around the state where many of the usually closed light towers are opened by the Coast Guard for access by registered attendee/members of the Association. More information on the Florida Lighthouse Association, their goals, and most importantly how your personal or family membership can support their efforts, can be found by visiting:

http:\\www.floridalighthouses.org

You will discover I have some strong opinions and I do take the liberty of expressing them occasionally in the text that follows. My concerns pertain to certain events that have unfolded and continue to unfold on Sanibel Island. To any neophyte "islander" who may wish to quarrel with any of my statements: I am allowed to express my opinions regarding Sanibel Island—I have paid my dues on her behalf—my wife, our children, and I are vested life members in the exclusive San-Cap B. C. Society. To qualify for membership one must have been a permanent full-time resident of either Sanibel or Captiva Island prior to May 26, 1963, the day both Sanibel and Captiva lost their identities as true islands with the grand opening of the first Sanibel Causeway. Suffice it to say, our membership roster is declining.

I would like to thank those who have helped expand my knowledge about the Sanibel Lighthouse site. The late Bob England (1920-2000) was the last official lighthouse keeper to live and serve at the Sanibel Island Light Station. Bob was an indispensable source to anyone who has seriously researched and written about the Sanibel light in the last 70 years. His wife Mae (1913-2005) also shared wonderful stories with me about their life at the lighthouse. Their daughter, Margaret, made family photos available for inclusion in this project. Betty Phelps, granddaughter of Assistant Lighthouse Keeper Howard Lowe, provided family photos and her grandfather's biography. The late Tom Taylor, a past president of the Florida Lighthouse Association, and author of numerous lighthouse books, reviewed some early, partial drafts of my manuscript and made some important suggestions.

The Sanibel Island Lighthouse is the most complete written work about the Sanibel Island Light Station to yet be published. Thus, I choose to use the term "A Complete History" as my subtitle. I purposely have avoided using footnotes and source citations because my book is not targeting readers who are structural engineers and academic historians. It is my intent for this work to reach the residents of Sanibel and Captiva islands who have a special bond to their historic lighthouse; visitors to the islands; others who live in the Southwest Florida region and may have an interest in learning more about the structure; and, lighthouse aficionados everywhere who enjoy tales about lighthouses and want to learn something more about their particular and individual history and operation.

The late Francis P. Bailey, Jr. generously gave me permission to use his family's Sanibel Packing Company postcards among the illustrations that are part of my personal collection and are used in this book. They are used courtesy of Bailey's General Store—Sanib'l.

Sanibel Island historian, Betty Anholt, reviewed the final manuscript for its accuracy in content and context. In the end, because of her input, at this time my book is the definitive available history about the Sanibel Island Light Station.

Sanibel Island—once known as Sanybel Island—and her nearby waters is a unique series of ecosystems. This barrier island is still a wonderful place to live or visit. To both the resident and visitor: I hope you enjoy your stay, however long. But, remember, no matter what our reason is for being here, we are only temporary custodians. I was blessed to live on Sanibel Island for most of my lifetime, and while I was there I helped take care of Sanibel for *you*, and for those who will follow *us*.

I dedicate this book to my friends who continue to live on Sanibel Island, to those of them who have moved away and now live elsewhere, and to the many who have departed and left me with fond memories.

—Charles LeBuff

Chapter 1

The Spanish connection . . .

THAT A JEWEL OF AN ISLAND EXISTED ON FLORIDA'S southwest coast was broadcast to the world in the 1517 logs of the Spaniard Francisco Hernández de Córdova. Hernández plied Florida waters shortly after Juan Ponce de León's expedition did in 1513, and a very special island would bring the Spanish back to this region repeatedly.

Juan Ponce de León and his crewmen are considered to be the first Europeans to have visited Sanibel Island. Many historians, but not all, agree he did so in 1513. Juan Ponce is almost universally accepted to be the discoverer of record of Florida. However, there is some cartographic evidence that suggests other Europeans were here before he was, and crudely mapped the region's coastline as early as 1502.

The Castilians, led by Juan Ponce de León, landed first on the east coast of the peninsula but were driven away by hostile natives. Their three ships moved south and days later entered the Gulf of Mexico to continue their random exploration. They soon made landfall again in Southwest Florida where his forces were attacked and driven off by a war party of Calusa Indians. At that time, the expedition's chief pilot, António de Alaminos, an extraordinary navigator from Palos, Spain, had decided the land was nothing more than a large island. Alaminos considered it to be just another of the Bahamas Islands chain. He and Juan Ponce named this beautiful, lush, newfound "island" La Florida.

The coast of Southwest Florida as Juan Ponce de León and members of his first Florida expedition saw it in 1513. The canopy vegetation consists of sabal palms and sea grapes. Noxious exotic plants, like the Australian pine and Brazilian pepper, have not yet reached the hemisphere. The white sand beaches are crowned with golden sea oats. This is exactly what Juan Ponce's "La Florida" looked like as his ships approached the Southwest Florida coast over 500 years ago. *Charles LeBuff*

According to existing documents Sanybel Island was next viewed by a group of Spanish slavers, led by Francisco Hernández de Córdova, in 1517. The chief pilot (navigator) of the Hernández expedition was again Antónío de Alaminos. Alaminos had arrived in the West Indies from Europe with Grand Admiral Christopher Columbus on his second voyage to the New World, and later he would visit Southwest Florida as a pilot in the company of Juan Ponce de León. But, this time Hernández was hunting for Native

Americans along the Gulf coast of Florida. Any Indians that could be were overpowered and captured during this shady expedition. They were to be enslaved in Cuba, Hispaniola, and Puerto Rico. Due to high mortality rates among the Indians already in servitude, because of European-introduced diseases, homesickness, and other causes, new sources of slave labor were constantly being sought. Kidnapped and enslaved Africans had not yet been brought into the Western Hemisphere in numbers. The Dutch would later introduce this enterprise.

An early Spanish chart of the Florida peninsula and adjacent land and water, from circa 1580. *Public domain*

Written records tell us that António de Alaminos remembered the location of the beautiful barrier island he had visited with Juan Ponce in 1513, so Hernández's party stopped there to collect drinking water at the same place Juan Ponce's expedition had. It would be marked on later charts as "Juan Ponce's Watering Place." Again the hostile Calusa Indians, who caused Juan Ponce de León to withdraw four years before, quickly set upon them. Alaminos and several other Spaniards were seriously wounded and Hernández would later die as a result of his injuries.

In 1521, Juan Ponce made a second voyage to Florida. This time he brought 200 settlers and a variety of livestock. He hoped to establish a colony on or very close to Sanybel Island. Some writers have suggested he landed at the present site of Punta Rassa, but 500 years ago Punta Rassa did not have any more room than it does today. In my opinion it is unlikely the tiny point of land had acreage sufficient to develop pasture and accommodate the needs of the colonists—Sanybel Island did, and its deep, protected harbor was not fringed with impenetrable mangroves like the shores of the neighboring islands and mainland were. The written logs of Juan Ponce and his pilots have been lost, so the exact site of this colony has never been determined. The specific location will be argued forever, or until the missing documentation is uncovered by a future researcher.

This second journey to Florida would also be the former governor of Puerto Rico's last excursion of exploration, for that year a Calusa Indian warrior mortally wounded him during a pitched battle between the cultures, somewhere near to, if not on Sanybel Island.

The Calusa were a powerful group of Native Americans. Their nation's strongly held and defended territory included modern Sarasota, Charlotte, Lee, Collier, and Monroe counties. They were primarily hunter-gatherers and most of their food items were fish, crustaceans, and mollusks harvested from the productive coastal marine ecosystems. At the time of Juan Ponce's final visit, the Calusa kingdom may have been home to as many as 10,000 subjects. Over the next half-century, following Juan Ponce's defeat, the Spanish feared contact with the Calusa, and consistently made it a point to bypass Southwest Florida. For additional information on the Calusa, I suggest you do an online search, and be sure to visit my website at:

http://www.amber-publishing.com

Click the link **Calusa Indian Art and Artifacts** to open that website.

After Castilian Juan Ponce discovered Florida, and claimed the land, it became the property of what was by then the consolidated Spanish crown and was governed by the kings and emperors of Spain for 250 years. During the Seven Years War (1756-63) the English captured Havana, Cuba, from the Spanish. After this war was concluded, and England was victorious, Spain managed to negotiate a trade. Spain conceded control of Florida to England, and Spain regained possession of Havana, Cuba. Under British jurisdiction Florida was subdivided into two parts: East Florida was controlled by a seat of government in St. Augustine; and West Florida, from its headquarters in Pensacola.

During the American Revolutionary War (1776-83) both East and West Florida remained loyal to England. Spain had allied with France, who was assisting the Americans, and Spanish forces captured Pensacola in 1781. After the war, during the peace-making process, control of both East and West Florida was granted to the Spanish. By this time, most Florida tribes including the remnants of the Calusa, had been Christianized and voluntarily fled Florida with the Spanish seeking freedom in Havana. (Isn't that a switch?)

Some groups among the Creek Confederacy, who had been supported and armed by the British, were forced out of Alabama and Georgia by the Americans and migrated south into Florida. These people distanced themselves from their Creek roots and became known as "Seminoles." The term was corrupted from the Spanish *cimarrón*, which translates in English to "runaway."

After the British government and its loyal subjects vacated Florida, the former English colony underwent a land rush when Spanish and American settlers hurried to colonize the region. Over time, the region was "Americanized" as more and more settlers from the new republic to the north moved into Florida, attracted there by the system of Spanish land grants, thus an availability of land.

Spain was later forced to transfer Florida to the United States of America in 1819 under provisions of the Adams-Onis treaty. This Treaty, between Spain and the U.S. required the U.S. to pay $5 million to its citizens who had valid land title claims against Spain. At the same time, as dictated by provisions of the Treaty, the U.S. relinquished its land claims in what is now the state of Texas.

During the second period of Spanish ownership the Crown had generously bestowed major gifts of land to special people. These grants were given for a variety of favors or services to Spain.

After the Territory of Florida was admitted to the Union as a State, in 1845, many of these land grants were tested in the courts to ascertain clear title. Much ownership was dissolved while others were validated. The Spanish land grant issued by King Ferdinand VII to the Duke of Alagon in 1817 was invalidated. Ultimately, most of Sanybel Island reverted to the public domain of the U.S. Title to most of the island would later be transferred to the State of Florida when the Swamp and Overflowed Lands Act was implemented, in 1850. This Act conveyed certain lands from the inventory of the U.S. Land Office to the states for reclamation purposes.

The name Sanybel can be best described as an Anglicized variant of the Spanish *Puerto S. Nivel* (translates to South Level Port) and was so noted on nautical charts early on by Spanish pilots and cartographers. More recently, some writers have suggested that the island first was named *Santa Isabel* by Juan Ponce de León to honor his daughter, Isabel. Another author has written the Ponce named the island to honor his queen, Isabella. Either of these feminine

Spanish names could have been linguistically corrupted over time into the island's current spelling, but from a more historical perspective the island's modern name is not considered to have originated with either romanticized origin. It is more likely that whatever place name was first applied to this flat island it was probably coined by António de Alaminos and not Juan Ponce de León. Unfortunately, the logs and notes of Alaminos—Spain's greatest pilot during the Age of Discovery—have not survived.

The place name Sanybel Island (sometimes Sanybell, Sennibal, and Senybal) first appeared on nautical charts and regional maps in the early 18th century and represents the original English-language name and spelling for today's Sanibel Island. After Florida entered the Union, the name of the island known as *Sanybel* was soon modified and over time *Sanibel* replaced the name on charts and maps. The Americanized name was in general use by the mid-19th century, but I find the name *Sanybel* continued to be published in relatively obscure scientific documents until at least 1896.

I should interject that it's interesting for new residents to learn that the proper pronunciation of the word Sanibel has been sometimes argued through time. In fact, this very issue was once debated at an early Sanibel City Council meeting. Florida natives, folks who were born and raised on Sanibel Island or live close by in Southwest Florida, traditionally pronounce the island's name as San-a-bull, not San-i-bell. So, from time to time when I'm writing, I like to use a contraction and spell the name as Sanible or Sanib'l. This is my small effort to help preserve the integrity of the native diction and traditional language. You may have noticed that I purposely used that variation of the word in my introduction.

The structures and beaches of Point Ybel have attracted visitors for more than 13 decades. The Sanibel Island Lighthouse remains one of the most-visited sites on the barrier islands. Until 1970 the entrance road to the lighthouse followed the Gulf beach. It was then realigned to the bay side to improve public access to the fishing pier and bring through traffic across the lighthouse compound to an end. When this photograph was taken classic automobiles are parked in the tiny public parking lot on the Gulf (They are identified as to make on the copyright page [iii]). Parking in the compound was restricted to government vehicles, official visitors, and the private cars of residents. *Islander Trrading Post.*

CHAPTER 2

Where once there was darkness . . .

THROUGH TIME, WISE LAND DEVELOPERS AND REAL estate brokers have used a variety of tactics to attract real estate buyers to Southwest Florida. Today, two of the more common amenities, which are used to attract prospective buyers, are the allure of waterfront and the open space of golf courses. In the second half of the last century, the "Water Wonderland" known as Cape Coral pulled would-be land purchasers to that soon-to-be city by the airplane load. Today, this sprawling canalized development is the largest city in population in Southwest Florida, and one of the largest, if not the largest, cities by area in the state. Much earlier, in the first half of the 19th century, speculating land developers likewise used attractive but more commercial-oriented amenities to draw distant purchasers into their sales web to help separate investors from their money.

At the time the New York entrepreneurs bought Sanybel Island, Territorial Florida contained eight lighthouses. These were administered by the Fifth Auditor of the Treasury, an agency of the Department of the Treasury responsible for lighthouses in the young United States of America. These lights were the St. Augustine (built in 1824), Pensacola (1824), Cape Florida (1825), Key West (1826), Dry Tortugas (1826), Sand Key (1827), St. Johns River (1830), and St. Mark's (1831) lighthouses.

Worldwide, in the early 1800s lighthouses were state-of-the-art aids to navigation. They helped fine-tune the coastal navigator's ability to position themselves, find harbor or port entrances at landfall, or avoid treacherous bottoms. Having a lighthouse at your doorstep leading to a seaport was definitely a valuable amenity. By its very nature a near-port lighthouse helped to encourage trade, connect domestic and foreign markets, and support inter-coastal commerce.

A civil engineer, named Edward Armstrong, of New York was commissioned by the Florida Land Company to create a conceptual map of Sanybel Island in June 1833 (Below). This map illustrates the firm's proposed development on the island. The economic enticement for those who would purchase land was primarily based on agriculture. The Armstrong map even describes the fertility of the soil on Sanybel Island in glowing terms.

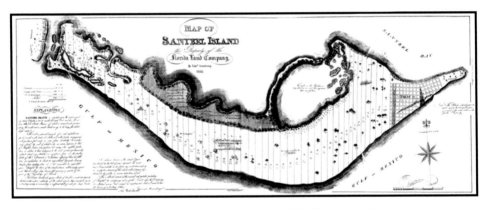

The Armstrong map of Sanybel Island from 1833. Prints of this classic map are still available for sale on Sanibel at the unique gift shop, Sanybel's Finest. *Charles LeBuff*

Three major land uses are represented on this map. Fifty contiguous parcels, each of which extended from the Gulf of Mexico on the south, thence north to the shore of Sanybel Bay (now San Carlos Bay), were platted on the western section of the island. Land immediately east of these future farmsteads was designated as "Town."

This proposed town consisted of 103, 400-by 400-foot lots. Some parcels were drawn as partial lots, because of their proximity to and intrusion into tidal waters. Within the boundary of the Town, 12 of the lots were designated as "public squares." Another series of six lots formed a triangle, also identified as public land. Another parcel, to the east of the town, was designated as a "common." This common extended west from the eastern tip of Sanybel Island for a distance of 200 "perches," or about 3,300 feet. Noted on the map are the words, "Intended site for a lighthouse." Apparently, the eastern point of Sanybel Island had not yet received a place name in 1833, for it is not identified. Fifty years later, the island's easternmost tip would be identified on charts as East Point and after another 100 years the point would be known as Point Ybel. More recently, some Sanibel Island residents have chosen to bless Point Ybel with the unofficial name of "Lighthouse Point." Along the U.S. seacoast "points" of land named "Lighthouse Point" are a "dime a dozen" and far from original. Point Ybel is a unique one-of-a-kind name and this place name should be retained for posterity.

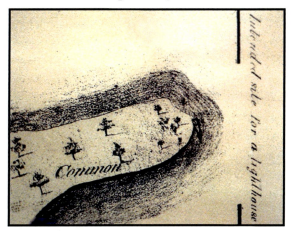

Today, the easternmost projection of Sanibel Island is charted as Point Ybel and is inappropriately known as "Lighthouse Point." This is as it is shown on the 1833 Armstrong map of Sanybel Island, with the future lighthouse notation on the right side of the image. *Charles LeBuff*

The petition requesting that a light station be constructed at the entrance to the Port of Punta Rassa later originated in Key West. At the time, Key West was, and still is, the county seat of Monroe County. In 1833 Monroe County included what today is Collier and Lee counties, too. The petition for a light station on Sanibel Island was officially forwarded to the Washington, D. C.-based Lighthouse Board in 1833. Ultimately, the request was denied, primarily because of an insufficient level of waterborne commercial traffic to justify its establishment. The start of the Second Seminole War in 1835 also discouraged settlers from permanently occupying Sanybel Island or other nearby barrier islands.

During this period, the U.S. Army built a series of cantonments along the Caloosahatchee corridor and scattered about the Big Cypress Swamp. Fort Delaney, at Punta Rassa, was built in 1836 and destroyed by a hurricane in 1841. It was the most westerly of these bases on the mainland. The Southwest Florida chain of barrier islands had only one army cantonment during the period. Fort Casey was built in the same time period on Useppa Island in upper Pine Island Sound east of La Costa (today, Cayo Costa). This fort would later suffer the same storm-related fate as Fort Delaney and was abandoned by 1850.

Fort Delaney would be reconstructed during the Civil War. During the decade following this war, Punta Rassa became a busy seaport, and it was only because of this commercial activity that a genuine need for a lighthouse would soon be seriously acknowledged and adequately funded.

The Sanybel Island development ultimately failed because of several reasons. The most notable cause for its demise was because of a legal decision. The courts ruled that the claims to the land, which had been included in the Spanish Crown's grant to the Duke of Alagon, were invalid, so any titles were nullified. Coincidental to the legal reasons, as mentioned earlier, the second Seminole War (1835-

42) disrupted the life of Florida's settlers. Policies of the U.S. Army, under command of General Andrew Jackson, thwarted settlers from occupying coastal islands, including Sanybel, and much of the wild lands of the southern Florida peninsula. Jackson was intent on re-settling Florida's Seminole Indians westward to the Indian Territories in Oklahoma.

By December 1856 the Lighthouse Board finally concurred and requested that Sanibel Island be withdrawn from the public domain and reserved for lighthouse purposes. Once again, funding was stalled, this time by the Civil War, and nothing happened until two decades later, in December 1877. It was then that a second request, further justifying the need because of the growing importance of the port at Punta Rassa, reached the General Land Office. Finally in 1883, Congress established the Sanibel Island Lighthouse Reservation and appropriated $50,000 to construct a lighthouse station complex on the island.

Documents purport that withdrawal of the necessary lands from the public domain took place through an Executive Order issued on December 19, 1883. This Order would have been issued by President Chester A. Arthur, but I have been unable to locate such an order for this date.

All of Sanibel Island and the northern end of Estero Island (Fort Myers Beach), or the tip of that barrier island known as Bowditch Point, were reserved for lighthouse purposes. It's interesting to note that during this same time a lighthouse reservation was also established on what is now Morgan Beach, part of the land known as Cape Romano just south of Marco Island in Collier County. The Point Ybel location was finally selected, likely because the Sanibel Island site was situated further westward and a light there would be more visible. This, coupled with the growth of the Port of Punta Rassa, resulted in the Bowditch Point reservation and the Cape Romano land eventually declared surplus. Since, Bowditch Point has become a park that is owned and managed by Lee County.

Before actual construction of the Light Station could begin on Sanibel, a land title problem arose.

A few years after Florida had entered the Union in 1845, Congress enacted the Swamp and Overflowed Lands Act of 1850. This act conveyed fee-title ownership of certain federally-owned lands to the states for drainage and reclamation purposes.

A cooperative Florida governor, William D. Bloxham, relinquished Florida's jurisdictional claim to the designated property, and Sanibel Island became a lighthouse reservation. Withdrawal of the necessary lands from the public domain took place by the above referenced Executive Order. Through the years, the U.S. has whittled this reservation down in size and has disposed of it piecemeal as surplus property.

The Sanibel Island Lighthouse Reservation was downsized considerably after the middle and western portions of Sanibel were released for homesteading in the late 1880s. By 1902, the western boundary of the reservation crossed Sanibel Island from the Gulf to bay two miles west of the lighthouse, about where Bailey Road intersects with Periwinkle Way today. That year much of the remaining reservation land (east of the cross-island boundary aligned with the present easements of Beach Road/Bailey Road) was surveyed into 10- and 15-acre lots. These would later be sold at public auction. By late 1923, the reservation had been reduced to its present size.

On October 31, 1923, the present boundary was approved by W. W. Himeritt, Superintendent of Lighthouses for the Seventh District, in Key West. The Coast Guard-controlled property, the Sanibel Island Lighthouse Reservation, now extends from the water's edge at Sanibel's eastern tip (Point Ybel) westward to the Gulf-to-bay north-south boundary. For cadastral surveying purposes, the tract's legal description places the line 1,000 feet to the west of the center of the lighthouse tower.

Chapter 3
When I first saw the Light . . .

MY FIRST GLIMPSE OF THE SANIBEL ISLAND LIGHThouse took place in December 1952. I didn't see it from the pitching deck of a vessel far at sea, but viewed its light from a more southern barrier island beach 11 miles away on the coast near Bonita Springs. Darkness had fallen and it's flash attracted my attention as it periodically broke the otherwise dark horizon.

Lighthouses had intrigued me in New England. I read in school textbooks about the heroic feats of lighthouse keepers and the personnel assigned to lifeboat stations. Both played an important role in maritime safety and navigation. Here, almost reaching out to me was a lighthouse. I learned it was on an island called Sanib'l, and better yet this was an island that anyone could *almost* drive to. Over the next few days, I was persistent and finally coaxed my new buddy from Estero, Don McKeown (1937-2003), to drive us to Sanibel Island the very first Saturday we could arrange to go. There's one important element here—neither of us had a driver's license; however, Don had access to a car. But, that's all part of another story (*Sanybel Light*).

~ ~ ~

SOME YEARS LATER, IN 1958, I was offered the number two position at the Sanibel National Wildlife Refuge. The refuge was established during the administration of President Harry Truman when a lease between the State of Florida and the U.S. Fish and Wildlife Service was executed on December 1, 1945. The refuge was not permanently staffed until April 1949, when William D. "Tommy" Wood moved up from Key West to assume the duties of refuge manager. At the time of the job offer, my wife and I lived in Naples, and I worked at the Everglades Wonder Gardens in Bonita Springs. The Gardens was a native wildlife attraction that had been started by two brothers, Wilford and Lester Piper, in 1936. For an interesting, illustrated discourse about its history visit the **Everglades Wonder Gardens** link on my webpage.

~ ~ ~

I ACCEPTED THE POSITION and in late December 1958 my wife Jean, our 10-week old daughter Leslie, and I made the life-altering move to the remote, wild island of Sanib'l.

One of the conditions of my employment was that we must live in Quarters 2 of the Sanibel Island Light Station. Tommy Wood and his wife, Louise, lived in Quarters 1. The U.S. Fish and Wildlife Service administered the Sanibel refuge. After the Coast Guard withdrew their personnel from the station, they negotiated a revocable lease with the Service which wanted to use the three quarters for employee housing and the land for other refuge purposes. The land would become part of the refuge, but the Coast Guard would continue to operate and maintain the automated light tower.

My family first moved into Quarters 3, a tiny two-bedroom cottage just north of Quarters 2, while I readied the former assistant light keeper's residence for us to move into. We were moved in by January 5, 1959, the day I officially started duty at the refuge. That we live in government-provided housing was a required condition of my employment. For the first few years our rent for Quarters 2 was $4.50 per pay period, or $9.00 per month. However, by designating one bedroom as a "transient room" for the exclusive use of visiting Service employees the rental was reduced by 50 cents and I ended up paying only $8.00 total each month. It turned out that I only had to provide lodging for two visiting refuge employees who were assigned to Sanibel on temporary duty—ten days total over the 21-plus years I lived there. By 1966 the rental rate began to rise about every two years. We had no air conditioning for the first 10 years, nor was telephone service available in those early years, although the refuge office had a telephone that used the lines installed by the Coast Guard during World War II. My employment with the Fish and Wildlife Service would span 32 years, until my retirement on April 1, 1990.

~ ~ ~

IT WAS A BLUSTERY FEBRUARY morning, in 1965. I was descending the stairs of quarters one, leaving the office of the Sanibel National Wildlife Refuge, to begin my day in the field. Over my thoughts I heard someone say, almost shouting, "Hey! Where's the lighthouse?" Glancing toward the parking lot I noticed a man standing next to a car. He had a camera hung around his neck so I assumed he was on the property to join the thousands of tourists who made an earlier, similar pilgrimage to Point Ybel to look at, photograph, or artistically paint Sanibel Island's next to oldest, still-standing landmark, on canvas. The oldest island structure at that time was an old oceanic cable terminal hut, a small building built in the 1860s as a link in the Punta Rassa to Havana, Cuba, telegraph cable. After composing myself to prevent a horse laugh, I replied, "Look up! You're standing next to it."

Since my family and I had moved into Quarters 2 of the Sanibel Island Light Station a few years earlier I had been asked virtually hundreds of questions about the historical light tower and its associated buildings. But, this was without a doubt the most unusual question I had yet been asked. I continued my tongue-in-cheek response to his question, and said, "If you reach out you can almost touch it! Or, just close your eyes, take a few steps, and you'll walk right into it!"

He looked at the brown tower, and with several slow nods he visually scanned the towering vertical object in front of him. Then, he turned toward me, frowned, and said, "Oh? I'm from the coast of Maine and I expected to see a *real* . . . a brick and mortar lighthouse!"

~ ~ ~

IN 1982, THE FISH AND WILDLIFE SERVICE vacated Point Ybel and relocated their Sanibel operations to the refuge's new headquarters on Sanibel-Captiva Road. Earlier, in 1979, while I served on the Sanibel City Council (1974-1980), I had discreetly worked behind the scenes to keep the Sanibel City Manager apprised of the timing of this move, and encouraged City Manager Bernie Murphy to become involved in the future of the lighthouse tract. In my small way I greased the tracks for the city to assume management of the Point Ybel property. In my view at the time, the city would be the best steward of the land and its vigorous historical preservation program would soon lead to the Sanibel Island Light Station's rehabilitation.

Now, 35 years later, until recently the two quarters were part of the city's Below Market Rate Housing Program. Selected city employees rented and lived in the buildings. Although maintenance of the two structures has been reasonably adequate there has been little progress in restoring the historical integrity of the station's compound or providing interpretation of this historic site for the tens of thousands of visitors who converge on Point Ybel annually. I am truly disappointed. Did I make a misjudgment . . . should I have covertly attempted to encourage the Florida Division of Recreation and Parks to apply for management of the land and buildings? They have certainly done a great job of restoring and interpreting the nearby Boca Grande Light Station. At this writing one can argue that the City of Sanibel dragged the anchor in what by now should be a world-class example of a U.S. Light Station.

~ ~ ~

THE REFUGE WAS RENAMED IN 1967 to honor the life achievements of Captiva winter resident Jay Norwood "Ding" Darling. In the 1970s, upper echelon management of the Fish and Wildlife Service made the decision that once a new, planned headquarters complex was in place on Sanibel-Captiva Road the Sanibel Lighthouse property would no longer be compatible with the refuge's objectives. At the time, I privately ranted and raved against this switch in policy, and after retirement I continued to do so publicly.

In retrospect, it seems to me the Fish and Wildlife Service has changed that position and today lighthouses are no longer deemed incompatible, expensive relics. They are now viewed as an asset to the interpretive mission of those refuges that have these historic structures as part of their real inventory. Today, at national wildlife refuges where lighthouses and other similar historic buildings exist, the structures and their historic roles in our American culture are interpreted as part of the refuge's series of important messages. The St. Mark's lighthouse on St. Mark's National Wildlife Refuge in Northwest Florida is a classic example of how lighthouses are today fitting in with the message and programs of a national wildlife refuge.

~ ~ ~

THE PHOENIX IRON COMPANY, of Phoenixville, Pennsylvania, near Valley Forge, was founded in 1812. This company made the wrought-iron parts for the Sanibel light tower and similar structures along the Gulf of Mexico. Wrought iron contains less carbon and slag than cast iron and is less brittle, so it is structurally stronger than the latter. The Phoenix Iron Company was a firm of high reputation and produced some of the finest iron in the U.S. during the 19th century. They prefabricated iron components for lighthouses and bridges, railroad track, and even manufactured cannons during the Civil War. In the latter part of that century they began to produce steel, but ceased all operations in 1984 after the American steel industry waned.

This is Sanibel Island's "sister lighthouse"—they are of the same design. This is the Cape San Blas Lighthouse on the Florida Panhandle. All of its parts sank off of Sanibel Island in 1884 and were recovered. Note its daymark—white with a black lantern room. *Charles LeBuff*

The light tower parts and the pilings for the quarters were to be shipped to Sanibel Island, along with another set of nearly identical parts that were destined for the Cape San Blas Light Station on the

Florida Panhandle. This cargo was transported aboard the schooner, the *Martha M. Heath*. In late April 1884, when she was about two miles off Sanibel Island's eastern point, the sailboat went hard aground, wrecked on a huge shoal that still extends offshore to the south-southeast from the point. The vessel broke apart, and most of the components of both structures fell into the Gulf of Mexico.

Two lighthouse tenders, vessels stationed in Key West, were dispatched to the scene. A hard-hat diver was aboard one of these boats. It has been reported that all missing parts except for two small fittings for the Sanibel project were salvaged by the diver and tender crews, with the assistance of the U.S. Lighthouse Service's project engineer and the contractor's construction team on Sanibel. Due to this happenstance, the tower assembly arrived on Sanibel Island behind schedule, but actual progress on the station was not affected. The light tower was completely assembled, both quarters were finished, the water system filled and operational, and the Sanibel Island Light Station was good to go by mid-August 1884.

The flashing beacon of the Sanibel lighthouse, the focal plane of which is elevated 98 feet above sea level, was first illuminated by a specially designed kerosene lamp—not too different in looks than what today is known as a "hurricane oil lamp." The size of a lamp was predetermined by size or, technically, the order of the lens, and that designed for Sanibel's optic contained three concentric wicks. This lamp was centered on a platform at the proper height for the outer optic's focal plane, and positioned inside the third-order lens. One of the curved panels of the lens was hinged to provide an access door to reach the lamp for cleaning and fueling.

Above are two third-order Fresnel lenses, similar to the designs that were once installed at Sanibel Island. The lens on the left resembles the first used atop the light tower. It has the round bullseye optics centered in panels around the focal plane. Such a lens assembly rotated on small wheels called chariot wheels and turned around a burning kerosene lantern positioned inside the lens. The bullseye prisms magnified the light and emitted the characteristic flash. The lens on the right is similar in design to the second Sanibel lens (see other photographs), but the focal plane (the wide prism) is centered and completely around the circumference of the lens. As the perfectly-timed acetylene burner, that was centered inside the lens periodically ignited, it produced a characteristic flash that was visible for 360°. *From the Internet*

These intricate optic designs were the brainchild of Augustin Jean Fresnel (1788-1827). He was a French physicist who developed the advanced optics technology that has since been used in most lighthouses around the world. Five manufacturing firms in France produced Fresnel-designed lenses for the world's aids to nautical navigation. Swedish companies also produced some excellent Fresnel lenses. Sanibel light's original third-order lens measured 5 feet 2.25 inches high and 3 feet 3.5 inches in diameter. The weight of a fully-assembled third-order lens, without the weight of the attached rotating pedestal assembly included, was about 900 pounds. In today's world, an optic of equal design and engineering specifications, with the same artistic craftsmanship used to create the original lens used at the Sanibel lighthouse, would have a value of over $3 million.

A third-order oil lamp, sans its glass chimney. This is similar in design to that originally used in the Sanibel Island Light Station. Notice the three concentric wicks. *From the Internet*

The Sanibel lighthouse in its work mode—doing what the historic structure was designed and built for in the 19th century. The light tower has been well described as a pyramidal skeletal structure with a central stair tube. Towers of this type were well-matched with regional severe weather patterns—they were more wind resistant. *Gary Cole*

The original catadioptic lens is believed to have been manufactured in 1884 by the French company, Henry-Lepaute. This firm worked closely with Fresnel and was noted for assembling the clockwork that were so essential to the proper functioning of Fresnel's lenses.

The Sanibel Lighthouse lamp was ignited, timed, and went permanently on-line the evening of Wednesday, August 20, 1884. The keeper on duty hand-wound the intricate clockwork with its complex gears coupled to a heavy descending counterweight. When engaged the counterweight caused the lens to revolve around the stationary kerosene lamp. As the clockwork unwound, the 115-pound weight slowly dropped a distance of 65 feet down through the drop tube, the pipe-like center stair support inside the light tower.

The clockwork pictured above is similar to that originally used in the Sanibel lighthouse. This one was used in the Cape San Blas light in North Florida, one of those installations known as Sanibel's "sister" stations—because the designs of the towers are basically identical. *Tom Taylor*

The keeper remained on watch throughout the night and was required to rewind the clockwork every two hours. After sunrise, the lantern was extinguished and the revolving mechanism disengaged and rewound. The 115-pound counterweight was then lowered onto an inserted support and the cable's tension relaxed to avoid fatigue on its strands. Next, the lamp's wicks were smoothed to ensure a uniform flame the next time they were lit. The attendant simply rubbed a finger around the wick; they were not regularly trimmed with a cutting instrument. Wicks were required to be replaced according to a written schedule.

The keeper filled a two-gallon container of kerosene from the large fuel storage tanks in the oil house, and had to lug it up the series of staircases. The air-pressure lamp used in the Sanibel light's third-order lens burned slightly less than two gallons of kerosene every night, or more accurately, 685 gallons of fuel per year.

Inside Sanibel light, 1998—Left, looking up at the spiral stairs from the bottom landing inside the stairway tube. On the right, looking down from the watch room level. The floor is at the upper right; the circular apparatus to the left is the base of the rotator pedestal that once supported a revolving third-order Fresnel lens. *Charles LeBuff*

Every facet of the lens and the glass lamp chimney were then carefully cleaned of fuel residue and soot. The keeper donned a long white linen apron so his buttons, belt buckle, or rough clothing would not scratch the glass prisms. Following this standardized daily cleaning procedure a white linen lens cover was draped over the lens to shroud and further protect it from the sun and dust.

Ten storm panes make up the glass-walled enclosure called the lantern room, at the topmost level of the lighthouse. Inside the lantern room khaki-colored, well-fitted cloth curtains were hung from hooks above the storm panes. The curtains helped to further protect the glass lens components from sunlight—direct exposure to which could heat the glass enough to actually crack the delicate and expensive-to-repair prisms.

Light keeping at the Sanibel light was equally shared between the primary keeper and his assistant. To reach the lantern room from the oil house at ground level, the attendant had to climb a series of steps. There were 15 from ground level to the porch; 19 from the porch to the lighthouse entry deck; one step up into the tube, then 105 more to the lens level—a total of 140 stair treads in all. The above stair count is contrary to what appears in many books and publications pertaining to the number of steps inside the Sanibel Lighthouse. The figures given here are correct. The total step number from ground level, excluding those inside the stairway tube, was modified from the original when the flights of stairs leading from the porches to the entrance platform were removed and replaced by a ladder(s).

After timing the light's characteristic with a stopwatch and making any necessary adjustments, the keeper would remain on station in the watch room. This is the windowless room beneath the storm-paned lantern room and is surrounded by the walkway platform and a set of railings. During the watches, the keeper inspected the lantern frequently to ensure that the continuity of the light was not compromised. Then the attendant rewound the counterweight mechanism on the required schedule. In this manner, the light's characteristic and brilliance were maintained night after night, year after year.

In 1912, an improved incandescent oil vapor lamp replaced the wick lamp. This new system was very similar in operating principle to today's gasoline-fueled Coleman camp lantern. Hand pumping forced kerosene into a pressure chamber where the fuel became vaporized. The kerosene vapor then passed through small orifices to reach the burning mantle.

The functional upper parts of a second pedestal assembly that was installed in 1912 is still inside the watch room of the Sanibel Lighthouse. A vertical shaft from the clockwork was fitted with a horizontal gear that matched the ratio of the horizontal hub gear (above). When the light keeper activated these they would turn the mechanism at the predetermined number of revolutions per minute. The outer housing, beginning at the lower end of the angled braces, and including the gear, turned. With its chariot wheels removed the base of the rotating lens was fixed to the upper ring that is supported by these braces.

As the lens rotated, flashes of light occurred when a bullseye prism came into a person's field of view and magnified the illumination provided by the inner oil lamp. The hub to which the large pinion gear is attached still revolves with ease when the mechanism is turned by hand. *Charles LeBuff*

Once lit, the lamp, housed inside the third-order lens atop the Sanibel light, burned constantly through the dark hours. Its lantern produced a constant 7,300-candlepower (CP) light. In other words, after the lantern was lit, it continually emitted that much of visible light. It was only when the rotating mechanism was activated that the lens systematically projected its amplified brilliance and a preset time sequence.

The original lens of the Sanibel Lighthouse rotated on a chariot wheel system around the centrally located lamp that housed the burning wicks. To anyone viewing it the slow turning, brass-mounted glass lens assembly appeared to create a flash. Actually, the series of magnifying bullseye prism optics, which were ground into the panels and centered at the focal plane, created the flash. These flashes generated 41,000-CP and were mechanically timed by the lens' speed of revolution and the number of bullseye prisms spaced in panels around the circumference of the lens.

This delicate mechanism produced a flash of bright light (41,000-CP) that had a 6.4-second duration, then 120 seconds of low-intensity light (7,300-CP) followed by a 6.4-second flash of light, again followed by 120 seconds of low-intensity light, etc. This interrupted pattern continued throughout the night. This regular flashing sequence was the specific identifying element of the Sanibel Lighthouse. This specific characteristic was published in the periodically released Lighthouse Establishment's *Light List* and on nautical charts of the day as: **FFlev.120sec98ftvis16M**. This designation means: white light, fixed (**F**), flashing (**Fl**) every (**ev.**) **120** seconds (**sec**) (the preceding is the "characteristic"), center of light 98 feet (**98ft**) above sea level, and visible (**vis**) from the horizon at sea level a distance of 16 miles (**16M**).

In 1923, the Lighthouse Service decided to phase out kerosene at its Sanibel facility and use acetylene gas instead. This required major change to Sanibel light's illumination source. For the Sanibel light keepers to take advantage of this improvement, complete refitting of the light and its mechanism was necessary. However, lighthouse keeping would ultimately become less labor intensive.

The first task of this conversion was to replace the rotating Fresnel lens and its bullseye prisms with a fixed non-rotating lens manufactured without individual bullseye optics in the central arrangement of lens panels. The replacement fixed lens, still a third-order, would accommodate a true flashing mechanism and produce a 360-degree flash.

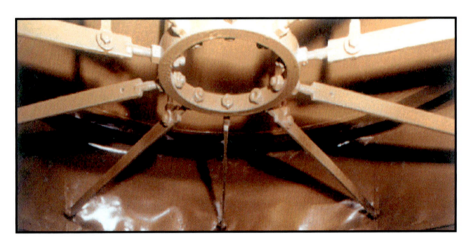

The original support (the spider) that provided an upper bearing surface for the revolving third-order lens is visible just below the ceiling in this photograph. This assembly aligned the top of the rotating lens during the 39 years it revolved. The spider is situated in the center of the room and its horizontal braces are bolted to the walls of the lantern room. Four vertical hangers connect the assembly to the ceiling for further stability. At the very summit of the tower's exterior is the ball-shaped ventilator and protruding from this is the precious metal pinnacle. These components are discussed below. *Charles LeBuff*

To accomplish the change, first two of the heavy glass storm panes and the metal mullion between them had to be removed. Through the opening, a long extending arm made from lumber was secured, and then a block and tackle was attached to the arm with its proper rigging lines. Then, sections of both sets of railings, the upper one around the lantern and the lower unit around the watch room, were removed. The individual lens panels were then unbolted at their brass-framed supporting petitions and doorframe. After disassembly, the delicate lens sections were slowly and carefully lowered to the ground one at a time via the block and tackle. The whereabouts of this lens is presently unknown. Apparently lenses were not well catalogued by the Lighthouse Service and later the Coast Guard. Both the first and second lenses may have been transferred to other lights that needed a third-order lens, but researchers have been unable to locate archives that suggest to what light station each was transferred.

The geared rotating pedestal from 1912, with its remarkable set of unseen inner ball bearings, was left in place with no connection to the fixed replacement lens. The pedestal would turn no more, except when moved by a curious official visitor, or maybe a painter doing regularly scheduled painting on the structure.

During my 24-year tenure (21+ as a lighthouse resident) working at the Sanibel Island Light Station the exterior of the tower was completely repainted three different times, the inside once. Sections of the exterior of the light tower are sandblasted if necessary and the structure is completely repainted about every 12 years. The inside of the light tower is not repainted as frequently.

Coast Guard personnel did the repainting work each time when I was stationed there. Sandblasting was actually performed only on those limited sections where rust and scaling was evident. The young daring Coastguardsmen sat in bosun's chairs and controlled their position by swinging about on secured lines suspended from points high on the tower. Their elevation was controlled by a crewmate who would lower them as necessary to reach the section they were working on. Some were experienced, others were frightened to death the first time they were lowered from the gallery. I remember one lad who screamed and came to tears, begging the stern senior Chief who was supervising the job not to send him over the side to be dangled and lowered. Before the project was finished all of them were as aerially agile as circus performers. Paint was applied with spray, roller, brush, and painter's mitt.

The iron pilings supporting the quarters were sandblasted and refinished twice since the 1940s; once by the Fish and Wildlife Service in the 1970s and again by the City of Sanibel with Coast Guard funding soon after the city took over the site's management in the 1980s. When the city repainted the pilings someone made the decision to paint them white, rather than the customary color to match the light tower.

In the 1990s a possible environmental hazard manifested itself because of long-term maintenance sandblasting. Over the years, repeated open-air sandblasting was a standard procedure to remove any serious rust on the structure. The lead-based primers and finish paints used in refinishing, before the development of lead-free coatings, often contained high levels of the metal. Paint particles loosened by the abrasion of high-pressure driven sand fell to the ground and mixed with the native soil underneath and adjacent to the structures. It is important to note that every time the light tower was repainted it was not always sandblasted, so the environmental issues were not as severe as the picture that was being painted. The most recent sandblasting of the light tower (before the major rehabilitation in 2013 occurred) in the late 80s saw the entire tower shrouded during the abrasive blasting to contain any airborne paint particles and reduce further soil pollution at the site.

At the time of refitting from kerosene to acetylene fuel in 1923, the flasher unit was one of only 10 such units in existence. It was a very progressive design that was state-of-the-art at the time. Six cylinders of acetylene gas (a highly flammable, poisonous, and colorless hydrocarbon) were hoisted to the base of the lighthouse staircase cylinder. The stairway begins its clockwise spiral just inside the entrance door and to the left. The tanks were positioned just inside the entrance door to the right of the central stair support which runs from the foundation, through the stair tube's base, and up to the top of the tower, ending at the unique rotation pedestal.

These acetylene-gas tanks, each weighing 225 pounds, were connected in a group of three to two manifold assemblies. At any one time, three tanks were active and three were on a standby manifold. A copper tube led from the active distribution manifold to the upper reaches of the tower and connected to the light-burner equipment. The gas supply tube was installed in the pipe through which the rotator pedestal's counterweight once slowly dropped.

Three new full tanks had to be installed, in rotation, every six months. For a few years after I arrived at the lighthouse, I assisted the Coastguardsmen in hoisting the heavy gas cylinders up to the entrance platform.

When their permanent personnel left Sanibel Island in 1949, the Coast Guard virtually abandoned the buildings to the elements. The wooden staircases leading to the lighthouse from each residence had deteriorated and were removed in 1951 by the Coast Guard. The Seventh Coast Guard District, headquartered in Miami, would not have to spend a dime to make any repairs on the station's buildings, other than the light tower, for over 30 years thereafter. When the City of Sanibel assumed management of the property in 1982, they successfully negotiated with the Coast Guard and received a $60,000 grant from the agency to re-roof, refinish the support pilings, and upgrade the interior of both quarters.

By the time I was occasionally assigned the fun duties of a light keeper, access to the lighthouse entry door required a climb up a vertical, 12-rung wooden ladder to reach a wooden platform which has since been replaced by one of metal. A Coastguardsman would stand on the platform and toss a heavy Manila rope over a higher horizontal member of the light structure, then firmly tie the line to one end of the acetylene cylinder in the bed of their pickup truck. The other end was secured to a ring on the bumper of the refuge's 1951 military Jeep. Then, with the Jeep I would pull the full tanks up to the platform and lower the empty ones to the bed of their truck.

During this period, the Coast Guard officer-in-charge issued me a key to the lighthouse—just in case someone, in an official capacity, should ever need one. By occasionally working on the lighthouse, I was the last federal resident of the Sanibel Island Light Station to serve as a light keeper.

The sun relay photocell was the main component of the light's acetylene illumination technology. Called a "sun valve," this apparatus was clamped to the upper gallery railing on the southeast side of the structure and connected to the ignition apparatus inside the lighthouse. The sun valve was invented by Gustaf Dalen of the Swedish company AGA in 1907. His device was the pre-computer-era "brains" of the light's ignition; it automatically turned on the gas flow at twilight and off at dawn, and it permitted the supply of fuel to reach the flasher unit. At dusk or during foggy conditions, the valve allowed the gas to flow into the pressure regulator properly. If it wavered out of kilter somehow, the keeper would have to turn and re-turn the small adjusting screws, sometimes for hours on end, to get the flasher perfectly synchronized.

Once all adjustments were correct, the acetylene light would flash 0.5 second, be off (eclipse) 1.5 seconds, flash 0.5 second, eclipse 7.5 seconds, flash for 0.5 second, eclipse 1.5 seconds—and so on through the night. The pilot light ignited and exploded at those frequencies as the regulated volume of acetylene filled the combustion chamber. Thus began the characteristic's all-night cycle. Then at dawn, light from the rising sun would close the valve and prevent the gas from traveling up to reach the pilot light inside the flasher chambers.

The flasher had three chambers. The upper chamber regulated

the duration of the explosive flash, and the two lower chambers regulated the frequency of the flashes.

These flash units were very delicate instruments. They could be very frustrating pieces of equipment, especially when they failed to maintain a perfectly regulated characteristic. The characteristic would never really be far enough out of synchronization to matter, but most light keepers were perfectionists. Small wedges would control the valves easily enough, but it could take hours to set the appropriate flasher chamber.

Knowing the original Sanibel Causeway would soon be completed and 24-hour accessibility to the light would become a reality, the Coast Guard decided in 1962 to electrify the Sanibel Lighthouse. Personnel from the Coast Guard's Aids to Navigation Unit at St. Petersburg arrived at Point Ybel with another lens and all the necessary fittings and equipment to make the change-out. The magnificent third-order fixed Fresnel lens was replaced with a much smaller 500-millimeter drum lens that had been once used on a long-obsolete lightship. As lightships were being phased out, these costly lenses were being recycled for use on seacoast aids to navigation.

They had one major problem, however. The Coast Guard detail didn't have a key to the lighthouse; they had forgotten it. To their surprise, I climbed up the ladder, pulled my key ring out of my pocket, and unlocked the door. Refuge Manager Tommy Wood had always told me to cooperate to the fullest extent with the Coast Guard, and for this lighthouse-related project he instructed me to assist in changing the lens.

The methodology, discussed earlier, which was used to remove the original rotating lens system, was also applied to this replacement project. Later, in the early 1980s, the lightship lens would again be traded out this time with a 190-millimeter beacon—the fourth lens assembly to shine at Sanibel light. The third lens to be installed atop the Sanibel light tower, the 500-millimeter drum lens, is now on display at the Sanibel Historical Museum and Village. It is mounted on a well-constructed but undersized replica of the previously discussed genuine pedestal that still remains in place high up in the Sanibel Lighthouse. The beautiful Swedish-made optic being displayed at the village is on loan from the U.S. Coast Guard. My hope is that one day it will be properly exhibited and interpreted at a museum in one of Sanibel's lighthouse quarters.

After electrification, the composite group flashing characteristic of the Sanibel light remained the same as in its acetylene-fueled days. Today, nautical charts code its characteristic and other information as **FL(2)6s98ft13M**. Also, the wooden ladder and landing at the lighthouse's entry were replaced with metal counterparts. Following electrification, the light's performance was plagued with problems. A series of standby batteries were included in the electrical circuitry because of the anticipated and already infamous power outages that occurred so frequently on Sanibel and Captiva islands. However, failures of such simple equipment as mercury switches and battery chargers resulted in the unattended light being occasionally completely inoperable for days and even weeks. Such is the price of automation.

The gong of offshore Number 2 bell buoy was also silenced and replaced with a new stationary structure and flashing light at the same position.

Another interesting aspect of the light tower's construction is not visible from the ground. There are eight skylights positioned around the circumference of the lantern room's metal floor. These are round and about one foot in diameter. Each contains seven hexagonal glass prisms. During daylight sunlight once flooded the watch room through the skylights so light-keeping chores could be accomplished. At night the lantern's glow provided light that was transferred through the same optics to dimly light the watch room.

The 250-watt clear glass incandescent light bulb pictured was once used in the lantern room of the Sanibel Lighthouse. These were the source of illumination between 1962 and 1984. A bulb-holding device held four of these and if one burned out another would rotate into position so the light could continue to function. *Charles LeBuff*

After 1949 the skylights were repeatedly painted over and were opaque until 2013 when the contractor rehabilitating the lighthouse removed the layers of paint. Light now passes through the glass.

When the light tower was rehabilitated in 2013 there was some discussion in the local media as to what the final color of the structure would be. It was decided and publicized that the tower would be painted its "original" color. The original color was apparently determined by decision-makers to be the brown color it was before the work started. This color is in no way consistent with the original color of the Sanibel light tower. In 1884, most of the Sanibel light was indeed painted brown, but the top was black. The top, everything from the watch room up, including the gallery rail around it, all the way up to the very tip of the pinnacle, was painted black. This color combination was the published daymark color of the structure.

In comparison one can see how such two-tone colors were applied by looking at a modern photo of the Cape San Blas lighthouse. The bottom of that tower is white and the upper parts (described above) are black.

Before we leave the construction features of this lighthouse, there is another aspect that warrants discussion. At the very top of the tower is a round-shaped ventilator and atop this is a thin, tapered rod known as a pinnacle. In simplicity, the pinnacle is one of Benjamin Franklin's lightning rods. It transmits electrical energy to ground through the metal tower whenever the structure is struck by lightning—and this frequently happens. Once in the late 1960s, during a fierce summer squall, I stood outside on the porch of Quarters 2 and watched and quivered as the light tower was struck by lightning 22 times. I wanted to document the frequency with which the wrought iron structure was hit.

The very tip of the pinnacle rod is made from the precious metal platinum, because of this element's ability to conduct electricity.

The Sanibel light is a seacoast landfall light. This means that it was not positioned to specifically caution mariners about hazardous bottoms or impending dangers. At night seamen who were sailing or steaming along the Southwest Florida coast were able to see the flashing Sanibel lighthouse more than 16 miles at sea. This distance as noted on charts and the *Light Lists* was the light's range line-of-sight from the center of the light out to sea level. The higher a person was situated on a vessel, the further out to sea the light's beam could be seen. After observing and timing the specific characteristic, a vessel's navigator could review their nautical charts and the light's compass bearing to determine the identity of the light and immediately know their vessel's relative position.

When looking up toward the ceiling of the watch room, the pinion gear of the rotator mechanism is to the right in this photograph. The two circular areas to the left are two of the skylights which once allowed light to reach and help illuminate the windowless watch room. Lazy painters, after 1949, over-coated the glass prisms and light was no longer transmitted through them, until the layers of paint on the glass were removed in 2013. The tightly spaced, narrow, barely stepladder-wide steps leading from the watch room up to the lantern room level are at the top of the photo. *Charles LeBuff*

About ten years after the completion of the Sanibel Island Light Station, the U.S. Lighthouse Establishment installed wrought iron, screw pile, range light towers in the upper reaches of San Carlos Harbor. During darkness, once an inbound vessel was in the main channel, between Point Ybel and Bowditch Point, the helmsman maneuvered to align the Front (outer) Range light with the rear range light. By keeping the higher Rear Range exactly behind the front light a vessel's pilot knew the course was properly aligned and following the designated channel. The 45-foot-high Rear Range displayed a 160-CP light and was positioned immediately south of the southern end of Fisherman Key. The 30-foot-high Front Range also generated a light of the same CP and was a few hundred yards to the south of the Rear Range, opposite Punta Rassa, near what later would become the ferry landing.

A large sea buoy anchored offshore marked the entrance to the port of Punta Rassa and the San Carlos Harbor channel. This bell buoy, Number 2, was anchored 4.75 nautical miles to the southeast of the lighthouse. Once an inbound vessel's pilot visually located the lighthouse or its flash, he next searched for the bell buoy marking the entrance, staying well to its east. The next act of navigation was to locate the front and rear range lights and carefully steer to maintain their constant alignment.

Before the range lights were erected, an inbound 250-foot-long cattle boat had difficulty in negotiating the channel leading to the cattle docks during darkness. Once the vessel's helmsman could see these critical lights or the distinguishing daymark colors of the towers during the daytime, he would steer a heading to maintain perfect alignment with the ranges. He steered under the skilled guidance of the Punta Rassa Harbor Pilot who had met the inbound vessel and had boarded her earlier near sea buoy 2.

The Rear Range was aligned visually by the helmsman, who steered so that the Rear Range stayed constantly directly behind the Front Range light as the vessel made headway. This way, mariners could safely negotiate the 12-foot-deep channel to reach Port Punta Rassa or the entrance to the Caloosahatchee beyond at night. Later, the Caloosahatchee would have its own sets of range lights. These were positioned at those points where the natural channel curved and was very difficult to negotiate in the dark.

In 1895, the characteristics of the range lights were: Front, fixed red; rear, fixed white. Like the lighthouse, these were fueled by kerosene. However, the range lights burned day and night. About once a week, the light keepers from Sanibel would launch their small light tender and cross San Carlos Bay to clean the lenses, service the lamps, and fuel these lights. They were each fitted with a large kerosene reservoir that surrounded the lamp chimney well above the focal plane of the lens.

In 1923, the Punta Rassa range lights were fitted with acetylene-fueled flashers and their candlepower increased. The front light produced 750-CP and the rear produced 2,500-CP. During the 1940s, the range lights were converted to battery power, and their characteristics changed. The Front Range flashed green every second, and the Rear Range had a one-second flash of white light every 10 seconds.

These prominent range lights were extinguished and their supporting towers dismantled in 1963 when their usefulness to local navigation ended. The lights on the drawbridge of the original Sanibel Causeway replaced them that year. Today, the lights on the causeway's new high span bridge, and those on the protective fender system of the main channel beneath it, now function as range lights for vessels that are inbound after dark.

~ ~ ~

ORIGINALLY, THE SANIBEL LIGHTHOUSE was accessible by one of four staircases; two on each quarters (one on the front and one on the back) leading from ground level up to the porches. Two separate stairways, one from each building, led to the platform at the lighthouse entry door. This staircase from the Quarters 1 porch was located on the structure's northeast corner, and that leading from the Quarters 2 porch was at the northwest corner of that building.

This design allowed access from either residence to the lighthouse. During severe storms and tidal flooding at Point Ybel, the crossover stairs permitted keepers to reach the tower to service and maintain the light. They also allowed the lighthouse-dwelling families to visit back and forth in inclement weather, or perhaps reach the safety of the light tower's secure staircase tube during severe hurricanes. In the fourth quarter of 1944, the latter was indeed the case.

It took a special caliber of person to become a light keeper, and a strong capable woman to become one's spouse. I should clarify that statement, here and now. Factually, most lighthouse keepers were indeed male, however, over the years there were a few woman light house keepers who had exemplary careers, some at stations far more isolated and arduous to operate and maintain than those staffed by their male counterparts. In the history of our federal career services there were few positions more exalted in the public eye than the dedicated and brave light attendants who lived on some faraway shoal or island and carried out their responsibilities for the safety of mariners and navigation of their vessels.

There were hardships and dangers to be faced on a daily basis at a light station. Illness, complications during childbirth, and traumatic injuries could be life-threatening. Spoiled canned food was once a major problem and whole families became seriously ill. In some instances medical care was many miles, even days, away. In the case of Sanibel it was about 23 miles to reach professional health care in Ft. Myers. It was a difficult trip to reach a doctor before the days of ferry service to the island. Keepers were well-versed in first aid and emergency medicine, and each station had a well-stocked medicine kit with state-of-the-art drugs of the day available whenever they were needed. During his tenure Sanibel's Assistant Lighthouse Keeper Roscoe "Mac" McLane died of appendicitis in 1938.

Since boating was an element of their job description and they regularly left their station to service lesser aids to navigation in nearby waters they had to be expert boatmen, even weathermen.

This photo, circa 1943, shows the two sets of wooden stairways which once led from the porches to the light tower's entrance. These were dismantled in 1951 and replaced by a wooden ladder. The ground-level cistern that is pictured to the left of center was later destroyed by the 1944 hurricane. Today, a single metal ladder gives access to the light's entrance from ground level. *U.S. Coast Guard*

During tropical storms and hurricanes the dedicated people of the U.S. Lighthouse Service, and later the U.S. Coast Guard light keepers assigned to the Sanibel Island Light Station were steadfast in their resolve to maintain the functionality of their light. Few American lighthouses ever faltered during storm events, unless a light tower fell from the impact of angry storm-surge water and the power of hurricane-force winds. Their quarters and the light structure were their only storm shelters.

Islanders could tell from watching worsening atmospheric conditions and the behavior of their personal household barometers that a bad storm was imminent. Many made their way to the lighthouse to ride out the approaching October 19, 1944 hurricane. This was at a time before these terrible and dangerous weather events were named and categorized by their wind speed. By today's standards this hurricane was a Category 4 storm as it churned toward Sanibel Island, approaching from the Gulf of Mexico. Fortunately, the hurricane dropped in intensity to a Category 3 by the time it made landfall. The islanders who came to the light station for safety

A medicine chest once used at the Sanibel Island Light Station. This is quite old, and was probably manufactured before 1900, because the plaque on the top (left image) reads U.S. L. H. Establishment, not U.S. Lighthouse Service. The right image shows the compartments which once contained pharmaceuticals and first aid supplies. When closed, the chest is seven-inches high, 9.25-inches deep, and 13.5-inches wide. *Charles LeBuff*

first sought refuge with the Coast Guard personnel and their dependents inside thequarters. The tidal surge was soon lapping on the main horizontal support beams under the houses. Fearing the buildings were going to collapse, once the sustained wind began to lessen as the storm's eye wall approached, men, women, and children crawled across the porches and up the stairways leading from the porches to reach questionable safety inside the light tower's stair tube. This was their refuge of last resort. Eyewitness accounts tell us that the tower actually swayed under the velocity of the high-speed winds although it was not designed to do so. The sound of the wind was said to be ear-shattering as it raced and howled through the tower's support structure. To communicate with one another people had to literally yell into each other's ears. Having heard those same sounds during lesser tropical storms during my years at the lighthouse I can personally attest to how frightening an experience it must have been.

The first appointed permanent light keeper at the Sanibel Island Light Station was Dudley Richardson. Dudley was already an employee of the U.S. Lighthouse Establishment and was promoted to serve as primary keeper of the Sanibel light.

A keeper's job was not a very secure position at the time and the rate of resignation was high. In 1884 the Lighthouse Board issued both formal dress and fatigue uniforms to their male lighthouse keepers. But, it wasn't until May 6, 1896, that lighthouse keepers became part of the classified civil service and a permanent career evolved after that.

The U.S. Coast Guard was given responsibility for lighthouses in 1939 during the administration of President Franklin D. Roosevelt. Those civilian keepers who wanted to could retain their positions, but on Sanibel Island the civilian lighthouse keepers would be systematically replaced by Coast Guard enlisted personnel soon after the outbreak of World War II, whenever there was a retirement or resignation. By July 1944 the keepers assigned to Sanibel would all have started out as coastguardsmen.

Between 1884 and 1949, dozens of men (there were never any women light keepers assigned to Sanibel), and in many instances their families, were assigned to the Sanibel Island Light Station. They were light keepers and assistant light keepers; at first employees of the U.S. Lighthouse Service (successor to the U.S. Lighthouse Establishment) and after 1939, they were merged into the U.S. Coast Guard. That year the civilian employees of the Lighthouse Service who wanted to remain in their positions were reassigned to the Coast Guard's roster.

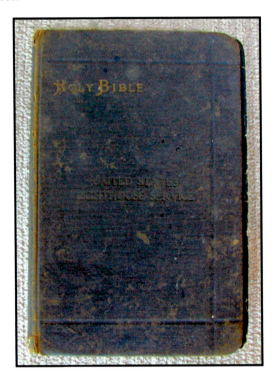

This 1903 standard edition of the Holy Bible was issued around the country to light keepers. This very Book probably comforted the light keepers and their families as they cowered inside the stairway tube of Sanibel's light tower during raging hurricanes. I used this Bible when I was sworn-in as a member of the first Sanibel City Council. *Charles LeBuff*

There are some published sources that list primary keepers and assistant keepers who served through the years at the Sanibel Island Light Station. I have extrapolated from those lists I have had the opportunity to review and added a few from my own independent research. I am listing them below to recognize each for his service, dedication, and for their contributions to the history of Sanibel Island.

It is obvious my list of light attendants who were once assigned to the Sanibel Island Light Station is incomplete. As mentioned above, there are a few partial lists, but like the others the one I provide has gaps in the timetable of those who served, and when, in each of the positions. At this writing this is the most compete keeper's list that I have been able to assemble. Few of the keepers left diaries, and few of their family members ever documented or shared their relative's achievements as keepers. Some keepers I interviewed had fond memories of their Sanibel tour of duty. It is also true that children of light keepers didn't always appreciate the experience of living on remote Sanibel Island. Many of them couldn't wait to reach adulthood so they could leave the isolated island, and then over time for many their Sanibel memories would become much more significant in their lives.

There are a few exceptions to the record, where descendents of Sanibel Island light keepers have later become lighthouse activists and carried on the legacy of their forebears, sharing their father's or grandfather's history. Two of these individuals are Betty Lowe Phelps, whose grandfather served as Sanibel light's assistant keeper from 1939 until 1944, and Margaret England whose father was the last primary keeper at Sanibel Island Light Station, serving from 1946 until 1949. I hope others will come forward and share their Sanibel Lighthouse-related stories before family photographs are lost and the rare written materials are discarded.

Betty's grandfather, Benjamin Howard Lowe (1898-1989) had a 15-year career with lighthouses. His preferred name was Howard. He started work at Fowey Rocks light in 1929, then moved on to light stations at Dry Tortugas, and American Shoals. He was transferred to Sanibel Island in 1938 to replace Roscoe McLane who had died. At Sanibel he was reunited with his family on a full-time basis, the periods of long separations were over. The Lowe family raised four children in Quarters 2, but after Mary's untimely death health issues forced Howard to take a medical retirement. Their youngest son, Roy, sometimes did what other lighthouse kids often did when no one was watching—climb the outside of the light tower hand over hand.

Primary Light Keepers	*Assistant Light Keepers*
Dudley Richardson, 1884-1892	John Johnson, 1884-1890
	Henry Shanahan, 1890-1892
Henry Shanahan, 1892-1924	Eugene Shanahan, 1892-?
	John Spencer, 1892-1896
	John Watkins, 1896-1897
	William Curry, 1897-99, 1902-05
	Baxton Lowe, 1899-1900
	Charles Gardner, 1900-1902
	Chester Roberts, 1905-1906
	W. Dewey, 1910-?
	Charles Henry Williams, 1910-1923
	Webster Shanahan, 192?
	Clarence Rutland, 192?
	Roscoe McLane, 1933-1938
Richard Palmer, 193?-194?	Benjamin Howard Lowe, 1939-1944
	Broward Keene, 194?
William R. England, Jr., 1946-1949	Malcolm Stogdill, 194?
	James Garner, 1949

The last full-time resident primary light keeper at the Sanibel Island Light Station was U.S. Coast Guard Chief Boatswain's Mate William Robert "Bob" England, Jr. Bob and his wife, Mae, and daughter Margaret, along with two enlisted men, were quartered at the Sanibel Island Light Station from 1946 until 1949. Later, son Bill joined the England family during Bob's Sanibel tour of duty. Because of damage to the facilities, and Quarters 2 in particular, during a 1947 hurricane, the Coast Guard determined that the site was unsafe for resident personnel. So on April 19, 1949, the light was designated as fully automated, published in the *Light Lists* as unwatched, and would no longer need constant care. The protective lens cover and the lantern shades would never be installed again.

Mary and Howard Lowe pictured in Fort Myers, in the early 1940s. Mary took ill and passed away on Christmas Eve, 1943, in the area's only hospital in Fort Myers. The following July, Howard retired from his Sanibel position and moved his family back to Key West. He would later move to Miami to live out his days, but he visited Sanibel on many occasions to check on the lighthouse and collect seashells. *Betty Phelps, from the Gloria Saladino family album*

Bob and his crew moved to the newly created Fort Myers Light Attendant Station on the Caloosahatchee, on the river-front just east of downtown Fort Myers. By the mid-1950s, this became a two-man station charged with maintaining the area's aids to navigation. By the late 1960s, the Fort Myers station was phased out and the aids to navigation group at the St. Petersburg Coast Guard Station assumed direct responsibility for navigational aids in the area—including the Sanibel Lighthouse.

Out of the blue, in October 1972, the U.S. Coast Guard announced plans to extinguish the Sanibel light. They had determined that the liPublic hearings were held. Many Sanibel and mainland folks voiced their opinions, arguing that the historic lighthouse should remain operational. As a tribute to the men and women lighthouse keepers of the former U.S. Lighthouse Establishment, as well as those of the U.S. Coast Guard who came later, the hearing officers agreed with the public sentiment. The Sanibel Island Light Station continues to "burn."

That part of the iron light tower above ground is in good condition for its age. As far as I can determine, the wrought iron footer pads that support the tower's weight and are attached with bolts to a buried concrete foundation were not uncovered and inspected for corrosion since they were first covered by sand during a hurricane sometime after 1923. They were flooded by corrosive seawater many times through the years. I have found one reference in a Lighthouse Service document from 1923 which notes they were to be inspected and cleaned. I assumed that after 88 years they were in need of serious maintenance. According to city officials with the Public Works Department who were responsible for monitoring the contractor's 2013 work, the pads themselves were not visible when the buried parts of the light tower were inspected in 2011. One pad location was excavated and the pad was found to be encased in concrete. When the pads were so encased is unknown at this time and the true condition of each also remains unknown.

The firm of Arnold/Sanders Consulting Engineers in Fort Myers inspected the buried section of the light tower all the way down to the concrete foundation and the upper reaches of the wooden pilings

The Lowe children are pictured on the Gulf-side of their Quarters 2 residence on April 18, 1940. L-R is Ben (Howard, Jr.), 16; Mary Louise, 19; Roy, 14; and Julia, 10. A year later, Ben would leave home and join the Coast Guard. The small pump house, which a severe hurricane would damage in 1947, is to the left. *Betty Phelps from the Gloria Saladino family album*

beneath that, on February 14, 2011. According to their report everything was found in "good condition." Earlier, I had arranged, through a contact in the city's public works department, to be present during this inspection. In the end, because of a change in the department's administrator, when the inspection happened, I was not invited to be present.

Another issue that needs attention is a section on the Gulf-side porch of Quarters 2. In 1973 the refuge manager authorized me to enclose part of this porch. It was justified to create more storage space, but I also used it as an office for my sea turtle conservation project, Caretta Research, Inc. According to the use permit issued by the Coast Guard to the Fish and Wildlife Service the exterior of the buildings were not to be altered. This project slipped through the radar and the cubicle is still part of Quarters 2. **It should be removed.**

OPPOSITE PAGE—Left to right are Bob, Margaret, and Mae England on the Gulf-side porch of their residence, Quarters 1, during their tour of duty at the Sanibel Island Light Station. In 2017, Margaret lives in LaBelle, Florida, where she worked as a elementary school library media specialist. She is a Certified Master Naturalist and leads birding tours at STA5 (Storm Water Treatment Area 5) and is involved with environmental issues in her region. *Margaret England*

The once well-delineated Light Station compound which contains the original lighthouse quarters and a brick oil storage building has become a victim of poor facility management. In 1972, following a change of refuge managers and the decision that the refuge would eventually vacate the Point Ybel property, the refuge staff was instructed to abandon the traditional labor-intensive upkeep of the grounds. Until recently, vegetation was allowed to encroach into the compound, which threatened the structures should fire occur. Much of the encroaching vegetation around the historical compound perimeter was taken out by Hurricane Charley in 2004, but it needs additional care. I was delighted when during the 2013 maintenance of the light tower all the plants that had invaded the area beneath it, over the 41 years of landscaping neglect, were removed. Fire has always been a serious threat to remote light stations.

Sanibel light does have a history of fire. The year is unclear, but it was likely in the 1920s that the station's quarters came close to becoming torches and being lost. Excess containers of kerosene were being temporarily stored beneath Quarters 2 and they were somehow ignited; most likely accidentally. The Light Station personnel started to fight the fire and luckily at the time, a Cuban smack was anchored in San Carlos Bay. Seeing the smoke, the schooner's crew responded and helped with the hand-force fire pump. Other Cuban crewmen formed a bucket brigade and dipped water from the Gulf of Mexico to fight the fire. The valiant efforts of Americans and Cubans working together saved the buildings.

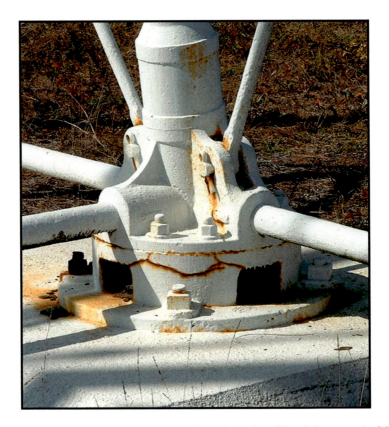

One of the wrought iron anchor pads of the Cape San Blas light tower in 2007. This is one of Sanibel Island's "sister lights." Remember, they even sank together in 1884. The only difference in appearance and general construction features is their distinctive daymark colors. One is now completely brown (Sanibel) and the other (Cape San Blas) is white with a black lantern room. Originally the Sanibel Island tower was brown with a black lantern. Everything you see in this photograph is completely buried by sand on Sanibel, and from my research and personal knowledge it is evident that none of its nine pads were excavated and inspected in many decades, until 2011. Even though the Cape San Blas pads are routinely sandblasted and painted this one is partially cracked and oxidized. It is interesting to note that the Phoenix Ironworks supplied two types of fasteners for this component. Old-style square nuts were used for the anchor bolts, *and* hex nuts were used to connect the base pad castings to the flange above it. The latter nut style was just coming into vogue in the late 1800s. *Iain Harnden*

A composite image of the base of one of the Sanibel Lighthouse supports after it was exposed by engineers during inspection of the buried structural fittings. These parts (lower turnbuckles and base pads) of the tower had been buried for the better part of a century. *City of Sanibel*

In 1974, the Fish and Wildlife Service covered most of the undersides of both quarters with plywood to reduce the amount of paintable surface and the time required for periodic maintenance painting. With their tell-tale burned lower corners rounded and charred by the flames, most of the floor joists were covered and are no longer visible. The outermost Gulf-side main support beam, which rests on the iron pilings, and the uncovered joists beneath the adjacent porch still show signs of the fire. Charred wood is visible from time to time where the paint is peeling.

Elinore Dormer exploring Pine Island in June 1972. The umbrella provided protection from the scorching summer sun. Ellie and I had earlier located and explored many of the old abandoned homestead sites on Sanibel as she gathered information for *The Sea Shell Islands*. This photograph was taken when we visited nearby Pine Island to investigate the whereabouts of a legendary stone that supposedly had been engraved at the direction of Juan Ponce de León. Ellie had uncovered some anecdotal information about this rock and wanted to try and find it and verify if the reports were true. We found many exposed limestone cap rock formations, like the one she is walking across—it is not sand—that day on the sand flats of western Pine Island, but none we examined bore any inscriptions or carvings. *Charles LeBuff*

Eastern Sanibel Island has no fire station in place at present to quickly protect structures at that end of the island. In the time it would take for the Sanibel Fire Rescue District (SFRD) responders to fight traffic on often congested Periwinkle Way, and arrive at the lighthouse in time to suppress a small but intense wildfire in the vegetation around the light tower, or even a fire that was accidentally started within one of the quarters, the quarters would be ashes. The buildings are tinder boxes and in the event of an accidental domestic-caused or electrical fire, the quarters would be lost for posterity. During my time at the Sanibel Island Light Station we constantly feared fire.

Now that the City of Sanibel owns Point Ybel perhaps the SFRD could investigate the possibility of negotiating the lease of a parcel on which to build a much-needed east end substation.

In addition, the Light Station's appearance continues to look untidy for a publicly-owned site and the traditional compound continues to overgrow. This certainly isn't in Sanibel's best interest, or conducive to the city's public image, because of what it conveys to residents and visitors—grossly neglected groundskeeping.

The overgrown-with-vegetation problem was somewhat alleviated on August 13, 2004, when Hurricane Charley slammed into Southwest Florida. Winds tore much of the high vegetation down at Point Ybel, notably the exotic Australian pines. During cleanup operations the City of Sanibel made a wise move and most of the surviving and still-standing pines were cut down and removed, but the Light Station compound is far from restored.

In the early 1970s, because of the light's significance to the history of Sanibel, the island's primary historian at the time, the late Elinore Dormer (1918-2003), nominated the Sanibel Lighthouse and keepers quarters for official historical recognition. By the way, Ellie's classic Sanibel-Captiva history, *The Sea Shell Islands*, is available for sale at the Sanibel Historical Village and occasionally in island book stores. She was successful in having the site so classified. So, on October 1, 1974, the structures were officially listed in the *National Register of Historical Sites*.

CUBAN FISHING SMACKS IN HARBOR.   SANIBEL, FLORIDA.

This hand-colored post card pictures Cuban sailing vessels known as smacks at anchor in San Carlos Bay in the 1920s. These boats were popular commercial fishing vessels and often sought refuge inside San Carlos Bay during inclement weather. Lighthouse Keeper Bob England provided refuge for a smack crew inside the lighthouse quarters during a 1947 hurricane.

Smacks, regularly fished the offshore waters near Sanibel and Captiva islands. They fished primarily for reef fish like grouper and snapper. The smacks were unique. The center of their hull was an enormous bait well. Fish were kept alive in these until they were processed for salting. The catch would be filleted and salted before they were transported back to Cuba. Following Fidel Castro's takeover of the Cuban government and the subsequent 50 years of silly ill will between the U.S. and Cuba this tradition was no longer permitted. *Islander Trading Post*

Kinzie Brothers Steamer Line operated a ferry service between Punta Rassa and Sanibel Island from 1928 until 1963. Pictured is the steel-hulled *Rebel* loading a 1957 Pontiac Chieftan at Punta Rassa. The *Rebel* was built in 1957 and had a capacity of nine automobiles. A round-trip voyage for two adults and their car was $4.00 at this time. Additional passengers paid 50 cents more each way. The first Causeway (1963-2007) had a round-trip toll of $3.00, but after the replacement second set of bridges were built in 2007 the toll rose to $6.00. *Islander Trading Post*

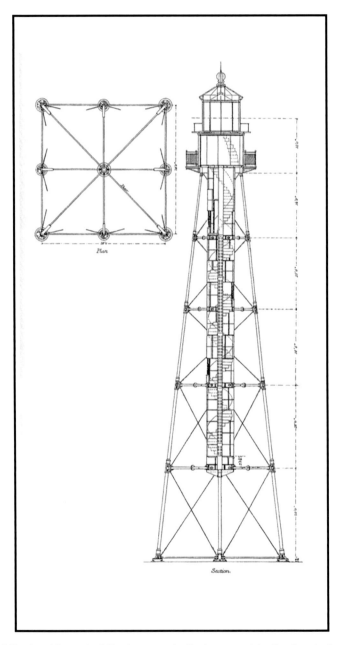

The architectural layout of the base pads that connect to the burried concrete footer (upper left) and the elevation dimensions of the Sanibel Island Lighthouse. *U.S. National Archives*

CHAPTER 4
Accessory buildings and their stories . . .

AT THE SAME TIME WORK CREWS STARTED TO ERECT the wrought iron light tower, workman started building the two mirror-imaged lighthouse quarters. These well-crafted wooden buildings are erected on a foundation of wrought iron pilings. This architectural design was selected to get the final finish floor level above the anticipated flood elevation. This was typical of how many of the U.S. Light Stations were built during the same time period along the hurricane-prone coast of the Gulf of Mexico.

The main part of each dwelling consists of four rooms. The inside corner of each of these rooms has an angled, plastered wall. This conforms to the center space of this part of the structure that is occupied by a large four-flue chimney. Each room had a cast-iron mantled fireplace vented by this chimney. These provided heat during the colder months, and they were fueled by coal. A closet was located in each room in the corners opposite the mantles. Four separate doorways interconnected each room, and the doors in each of the four rooms opened onto the north and south porches.

The floor plan of each wing originally consisted of a kitchen with its own chimney and an adjoining storage room. The porch area between the main living section and kitchen wing was originally an open-air breezeway, at the southern end of which was situated a laundry sink and next to that a "one-holer" toilet closet—also known, usually when not connected to a main residence, as an outhouse. In 1923 the storage areas next to the kitchens were modernized and became bathrooms. At the same time both ends of the breezeways were enclosed and had an exterior door installed at each end. Fine mesh, bronze, sand fly (no-see-ums) resistant screen enclosures were also added in 1923 on the bayside corners of each porch—on those ends opposite the flight of stairs leading up to the lighthouse entrance. Thereafter the privy closet was used for storage. The screen enclosures were dismantled in 1969 by the Fish and Wildlife Service.

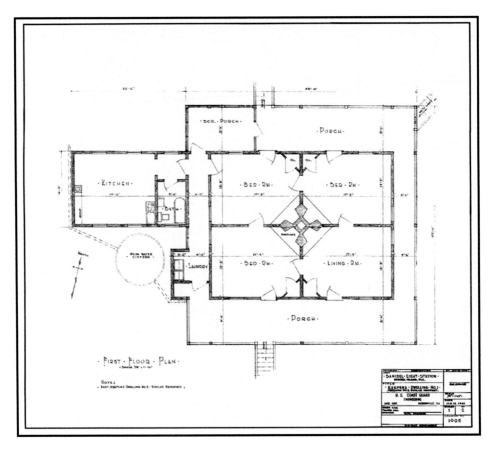

OPPOSITE PAGE—Floor plan—Quarters 1—Sanibel Island Light Station. As mentioned in the note on this print, the floor plan of Quarters 2 is a mirror image of the above layout. In 1941, the residence was utilized as shown, but after the front stairs were torn away by a hurricane in 1947 the living room was relocated to the upper left bedroom to better serve as an entrance. The brick base of the rainwater cistern remains, but the wooden tank itself dried out and made an explosive sound when it collapsed, in 1976. I salvaged some of the best wood and made some nice picture frames from the tank's beautiful cypress lumber for my children. *Public domain*

Elevations—Quarters 1.. As mentioned on the above print, the elevations of Quarters 2 are mirror images of this layout. The front elevations give the dimensions for the quarter's ceilings as 12-feet, 6-inches. The ceilings of the kitchen wing were 10-feet high. *Public domain*

One of the cast-iron fireplaces used to heat the Sanibel lighthouse quarters. The grate is removable and this is where coal was originally stoked to provide heat for the structure. One of these fireplaces was located in each room of the main section of both quarters. Each structure's kitchen wing had its own chimney to vent a stove which was used for cooking, and when needed, heating. Collectible Sanibel Lighthouse memorabilia sets on this mantle and a three-dimensional metal sculpture of the complex is mounted on the plastered brick wall. *Charles LeBuff*

The painted walls and ceilings of the quarters are four-inch wide well fitted, tongue-and-groove pine boards. The flooring is of similar lumber but when we moved in it had been over-coated with a Sherwin-Williams product, a premixed dark walnut-stain and gloss varnish combination. The original ceilings in the living area are 12-feet-6-inches high, while those in the kitchen wing are 10-foot high. After the Fish and Wildlife Service left Point Ybel city employees living in Quarters 2 sanded off the varnish stain and then refinished most of the flooring with a clear topcoat.

Periodically, light-tending vessels would arrive from Key West to deliver staple commodities to personnel and parts and fuel for operation of the lighthouse. Kerosene lamp fuel was first stored in a small frame building at the foot of the light tower. This building was replaced in 1894 with one made from brick. This is the oil house that stands on the site today. I made the existing (2017) sandblasted wooden sign fixed to the structure in my sign shop that I operated on Sanibel from 1965 until 2004. When I contracted the job I advised the procurer that the old wooden sign that was attached to the brick wall at the time incorrectly stated the structure is ten years older than it really is. The incorrect date was perpetuated on the replacement sign.

During World War II the threat of saboteurs who might disembark from German submarines concerned our government. After the start of the war, the Coast Guard was put under the control of the U.S. Navy for the duration. A national Beach Patrol Division was created in 1942, and the Coast Guard was assigned the responsibility of building a nationwide network of coastal observation and patrol bases to thwart possible clandestine enemy infiltration. The 24,000 personnel who were assigned to the beach patrol units became known as "sand pounders" because they hiked along beaches. These posts were responsible for guarding our seaports and coastline from invasion and to prevent enemy agents from communicating to or from our shores.

The nearly 50-year old Sanibel lamp oil storage building as it appeared in 1943. The roof at the time was corrugated steel—it is currently covered with asphalt/fiberglass shingles. Whenever rehabilitation of the Light Station begins, the roof covering should be restored to its original style. When light keepers last utilized the oil house routinely it contained tanks of kerosene from which the fluid was dispensed and then hand-carried aloft to fuel the lamp inside the original revolving third-order lens. The perimeter fence of a single two-inch pipe mounted on stout cypress posts, that delineated the light station compound, is still in place in this photo and the small Australian pines were being well-maintained. *U.S. Coast Guard*

In 1942, the Coast Guard's Beach Patrol constructed a two-bedroom cottage on Sanibel. This would later become lighthouse Quarters 3, after the War ended and the patrol units were disbanded. A wooden tower was also erected out on the extreme eastern tip of Point Ybel in 1942.

The Sanibel Island Light Station as pictured in 1949. This photo was taken not long after the U.S. Coast Guard had vacated the station and about the time the Fish and Wildlife Service took over the buildings and land management. The structures, from left to right, are: The World War II observation tower, Quarters 2 and 3 (notice the windows in the quarters have their storm shutters in place, screened porches, and the elevated water tanks are situated between the two quarters). Prominent in the light tower is the enormous third-order stationary Fresnel lens. The oil house and the Beach Patrol cottage are also pictured. Depending on erosion and the tidal level at Point Ybel, periodically the concrete footers of the observation tower are exposed as are bricks from the cottage's chimney. The former was burned down in 1960 and the latter was bulldozed and buried on the beach, in 1969. *U.S. Coast Guard*

The Sanibel Island Light Station already headquartered the light-keeping staff, and the station's personnel had no administrative connection to the newly organized coastal patrol agency. The Coast Guard's Aids to Navigation Division gave permission for the Beach Patrol Division to use some land and they constructed the cottage to house their patrolmen. Regulations prevented the lighthouse tower from being used for observation purposes, so they built the 35-foot tall observation tower. From this vantage point lookouts maintained surveillance of the channel entrance to the port of Punta Rassa. The special detachment of coastguardsmen assigned to Sanibel Island during the War also patrolled the beaches of Sanibel and Captiva by Jeep, looking for enemy landings. The enemy was never encountered on island beaches, but U-boat traffic was indeed real in the Gulf of Mexico and merchant vessels were torpedoed and sunk offshore. It is rumored that a German submarine sank somewhere west of Gasparilla Island, where Port Boca Grande used to be. A German U-boat sank the merchant vessel *Baja California* in 1942. She lies in 110 feet of water about 55 miles south of the Sanibel Lighthouse.

In June 1942, German submariners successfully deployed a group of four saboteurs. These men landed on Florida's East Coast, south of Jacksonville. Thanks to observant Americans these men were quickly captured. They were promptly tried and condemned by military tribunals and were executed by use of the electric chair.

OPPOSITE PAGE—Lighthouse Quarters 3, in 1943. This two-bedroom cottage was built in 1942 to house beach patrolmen. My family and I lived here for a week in 1959. By that time, hurricanes had pushed in about two-feet of sand and there was only about 10-inches of clearance between the earth and the perimeter beam of the concrete foundation. The Fish and Wildlife Service used this as a vacation rental unit for Service employees. In 1959, the rental rate was $.96 per night, by the time its motel role ended in 1967 the cost had soared to two dollars per night—reservations were capped at a one-week stay. We razed the building with a bulldozer in 1969 and it was buried in a pit dug in the nearby beach. From time to time, depending on erosion, the bricks of the chimney and some of the tile faced concrete floor are exposed out on the Point Ybel beach. *U.S. Coast Guard*

The various military personnel assigned to this Sanibel-based operation and the lighthouse had an enjoyable tour of duty and most of them quickly fell in love with the place despite the element of isolation. In fact, many veterans who were assigned to Sanibel during World War II, or who were trained at nearby regional military airfields, resettled in Southwest Florida after the War ended in 1945. Some later retired to Sanibel Island, others came earlier and started new careers here.

In May 1884, when the lighthouse construction commenced on Sanibel, a 165-foot-long wharf had already been built on the bay side of Point Ybel. It was ready to accommodate offloading construction equipment and material. A few years later, this pier was downsized and a roofed superstructure was added to it. This covered davits that were used to lift small vessels out of the water and provide protected storage for the small boats. By 1923, at the location where this pier's wooden deck touched dry land, it connected to a broad concrete walkway that led south toward the oil house. Before reaching that structure it forked and continued on either side of the oil storage building where it terminated at the foot of each quarters stairway. In the early 1930s each side of the walk was landscaped with introduced Australian pines. These were kept trimmed—almost in a topiary fashion. After the Coast Guard vacated the station the pines were no longer manicured and were allowed to grow throughout the property. That is, except those that sprouted in the station's compound or on the beach to obscure the view. In the 1950s and 1960s we periodically pulled these out by hand or with the refuge Jeep.

Three exposed concrete footers from the Coast Guard's World War II observation tower were still visible during low tide at Point Ybel in 2007. As of this writing, in 2017, all four are uncovered by sand. *Charles LeBuff*

On the bay and paralleling the pier walkway, just to the east and next to it, was an elevated sloping marine railway. The lower end of the rails extended underwater into San Carlos Bay. The larger motor vessel assigned to the light station could be floated onto a submerged dolly and then winched clear of the water on this boat ways and into the enclosed boathouse a few yards from the water's edge for dry storage. The Fish and Wildlife Service had no use for the structure and because it had fallen into major disrepair I was ordered to demolish it in 1960.

After the Coast Guard left Sanibel, in 1949, the Australian pines along the walkway were never trimmed or maintained in any way again. They grew rapidly and by the turn of the 21st century they had attained a height nearly equal to that of the light tower. Hurricane Donna (1960) thinned them somewhat, but Hurricane Charley (2004) and its aftermath cleanup finished them off. I was very pleased to have Nature help "restore" the vegetative composition of Point Ybel.

This early photograph, from circa 1900, captures people that were visiting the Sanibel Island Light Station. One of the local steamships of the day; perhaps the *Dixie* or *Uneeda* dropped them off at the Lighthouse Service dock for a closeup peek of the lighthouse and some shelling on the Point Ybel beaches. *Public Domain*

PREVIOUS PAGE—At the center of this 1913 poor quality, real photo postcard image is the bayside boathouse and the angled marine railway discussed above. The boathouse at the far right was destroyed by a major hurricane in 1926 and later replaced by a structure with a roof only, without sidewalls, which housed a manual davit system. *Islander Trading Post*

A later photo, from circa 1933, shows the Sanibel Island Light Station from an aerial perspective. The well-manicured compound is clearly discernible, as is the walkway from the pier. Small, trimmed Australian pines line both sides of the concrete walkway. Most of these trees were still in place in 2004 when the winds of Hurricane Charley slammed into Sanibel Island. The hurricane toppled the majority of them. During the aftermath cleanup, most of these remaining exotic plants were removed from the Coast Guard property by the city. *U.S. Coast Guard*

In 1947 the station was damaged by a major hurricane. Tropical cyclones were unnamed in those days. In this photo we find the Gulf-side stairway of Quarters 2 has been torn away and the pumphouse door is missing. The Gulf-front stairway of Quarters 1 was also swept away and neither of these flights of stairs were ever replaced. Vegetative debris has been hurled underneath the structure by wind and waves. A 4,000 gallon metal cistern that connected to Quarters 2 before the hurricane, which had replaced the cypress tank after a 1944 hurricane, disappeared in the storm and was never replaced. A temporary tidal pool has formed at its former location just beyond the coconut trees. *State Archives of Florida*

The Sanibel Island Light Station during a tidal surge in 1959. The compound is flooded by shallow seawater. This is a result of the glancing blow of a tropical weather system and the combined forces of high tide and the storm-created-surge. In 2017 the elevation of the ground at the base of the light tower is five feet above mean sea level. At this writing it is more than a foot higher than what existed during construction in 1884. The highest natural elevation on Sanibel Island is a small section of Gulf beach ridge which barely exceeds 13 feet above sea level. Storms have brought volumes of sand and shell ashore at the lighthouse over the decades. Point Ybel continues to erode at its tip and along its San Carlos Bay shoreline. *Islander Trading Post*

Chapter 5
Plumbing and other utilities . . .

On most coastal barrier islands, Sanibel-size or smaller, adequate supplies of potable water were a luxury for residents. Inadequate supplies restricted or even prevented settlement and development. However, Sanibel was different from most other barrier islands because potable water was an available, easily used, and most reliable natural resource. Prior to permanent settlement of Sanibel Island by the general American citizenry after 1888, year-round surface freshwater, hydrologically known as the water-table aquifer was very restricted. It was hydraulically connected at the surface only during, and for a few months after the end of, the summer rainy season. By mid-winter, the surface volume of sweet water had receded and freshwater existed only at a few scattered, shallow ponds that were actually created and maintained by alligators. By late spring, when drought conditions commonly prevailed, the only freshwater that was left at the surface existed in a few of those alligator holes that were deep and were located in the small open areas subject to annual seasonal rain flooding.

On Sanibel, the surface water-table aquifer penetrates the Earth's crust to a variable depth, depending on how deep the nearly impermeable clay deposit is at its base. The maximum depth of this supply of surface water is around 25 feet below the island's surface.

Recently, this aquifer has been referred to as a "lens" of freshwater, and its very existence means that Sanibel is nearly unique among Florida barrier islands. Still deeper, below the surface water, there are other layers (aquifers) of water that are saltier. This means that they have higher sodium chloride and other salt concentrations. The uppermost of these is called the shallow artesian aquifer. This layer lies below the clay layer and atop a limestone stratum. Sometimes referred to as bedrock, the limestone layer varies in depth, but generally the uppermost level of this deposit lies between 29 and 34 feet beneath the island's surface. This limestone, some of which is water-bearing, varies in thickness and is believed to totally underlie Sanibel. In some areas, it extends to a depth of 130 feet. The clay layer is a barrier, positioned above the shallow artesian aquifer. Unless it is penetrated by wells or excessively deep surface excavations it prevents the brackish artesian water from intruding into the upper freshwater lens.

Several hundred feet below the shallow artesian aquifer is another stratum of water known as the deep artesian aquifer. The uppermost part of this is called the lower Hawthorn aquifer. These two artesian aquifers are separated by a variety of limestone, clay, phosphoric sand, and marl deposits. Marl is a mixture of several of the soil types. Still deeper are other water-bearing formations, but these are beyond the scope of this discussion. The deep artesian aquifer is under such extreme subterranean pressure that water is dispersed vertically and horizontally through the porous limestone earth. If this water-impregnated layer is penetrated by a well, the well is supplied by pressurized water that is ejected up to a level, or artesian head, that is often a considerable number of feet above the Earth's surface.

All well-constructed residences on post-1900 Sanibel Island (that is, those that were not simple palm-thatched dwellings, as many were) included one or more cisterns. These cypress-staved or shell-concrete tanks were connected to the structure's roof by gutters and downspouts. Precipitation falling on the roofs was the source of water unless pumping potable water from a well could augment the roof-supplied cistern water. Two major types of shallow wells penetrated the ground at selected locations into the surface-water aquifer. The first were permanent shallow pits that were hand-dug by those homesteaders who were fortunate enough to have built their houses on high ridges where cabbage palms grew in abundance. The presence of these trees meant to the pioneers that fresh potable water existed just a few feet below (this was the same technology used by the early Spanish visitors). The pits, some of which were 6-feet square and 5 feet deep, were often lined with brick or concrete to prevent the soil from sloughing in. Having percolated through the permeable soil, freshwater from the water table-aquifer would seep in, filling the excavations and maintaining its level in these shallow wells.

Some housing units, such as the Palms Hotel which was once located just to the west of the lighthouse reservation boundary, had a windmill-driven pump to force the water into raised wooden water storage tanks. The Palms Hotel was owned by the Shanahan family, some of whom were former Sanibel light keepers, and it burned down in 1936. These tanks were usually separate from the cistern system. Turn-of-the-century (19th/20th) residents and farmers who could afford them had wells drilled into the deep artesian aquifer. Under ideal conditions, the pressurized water first entered an aeration tank to help diffuse the sulfur dioxide gas dissolved in the water into the atmosphere and thus remove the poor taste and odor (rotten eggs) of the water. Before electricity came to the islands and electric pumps were available, the water was forced by windmill or hand pumped into an elevated tank that supplied gravity-fed water to the buildings. With water originating from the heavens (rain) or from just a few feet below the Earth's surface, water conservation was almost always an important element of island living. Generations of people reared on Sanibel and Captiva islands were guided by one simple doctrine: "*On this island in the sun, we don't flush for number one.*"

When the Sanibel Island Light Station was completed, it included a state-of-the-art water system (at least for lighthouse complexes established on remote subtropical barrier islands). A 4,000-gallon elevated cistern was located on the Gulf side of each living quarters where the kitchen wing joined the house. The bottoms of the tanks were raised about 8 feet off the ground on stout, round, and thick brick bases. These water reservoirs were made of full 2-inch-thick, 4-inch wide, vertical cypress staves. Each board was expertly beveled at its edges so when fitted together they formed a perfect watertight circular tank. These were bound in place with seven 1/2-inch-round, adjustable metal straps around the cistern's circumference. A similar, slightly larger 5,000-gallon cypress tank was built and held together in the same manner. It was placed between the buildings at near ground level and rested on driven foundation pilings. In those days, the light station's potable water was indeed heaven-sent. Each downspout allowed rainwater, falling on the roofs and carried about by the guttering, to flow into the cisterns.

There were two downspouts running into each tank, and each had a movable butterfly valve. During dry times when rain was imminent, these valves were adjusted so the rain was diverted from entering the cisterns. After sufficient rain had fallen to clean the roofs, gutters, and cistern-connecting pipes, the valves were repositioned so that rainwater entered the tanks again. This technique washed away any bird droppings, dead insects, or any other undesirables that had fallen onto the roofs since the last cleaning. During the summer rainy season, with almost daily rains, the butterfly valves remained adjusted so rainfall entered the system without further cleaning of the roofs. The only potable running water serving the dwellings was supplied via a direct line from their respective cisterns into the kitchens. The ground level 5,000-gallon tank was a backup system. Its contents could also be pumped up to either of the raised cisterns when necessary. From time to time, water was brought to the station aboard regularly visiting lighthouse-tender vessels and pumped to top off the tanks. From 1884 until 1923, there was no other plumbing in the quarters.

Quarters 2, in 1943, with the dwelling's cistern and downspouts in place. Even a dog house is close to the tank's circular red brick base. Two downspouts lead from the large gutters into the top of the tank. The original privy is also pictured here, sans chute. It is located to the left of the cistern, between the vertical board and the corner. The front stairs are visible and someone has had a busy washday. *U.S. Coast Guard*

Privies (outdoor unplumbed pit toilets), which were used every day, were located on the upper beach on the Gulf side of the dwellings. Each residence also had a privy closet on a porch. These were located on the outer Gulf-side part of the structure not far from the corners where the elevated cisterns stood. These were boxed, completely enclosed by a wooden vertical chute, all the way down to a pit in the ground. These primitive toilets were used when weather or mosquitoes made it impossible to leave the buildings. Then in 1923, major improvements were made to the Light Station's quarters and plumbing facilities. Prior to that time, the kitchen wing was separated from the four-room section by an open breezeway. Remodeling included closing in the breezeway and constructing screen porches on the bayside of each building. I removed both screen enclosures in the late 1960s. "Real" bathrooms were installed in each living quarters in the area that formerly was a combination pantry and storage room. The fixtures included bathtubs, flushing toilets, and sinks.

Two 30-foot-high elevated water towers were built between the houses. Each of these supported a 1,000-gallon cypress tank. The tanks were covered similarly to the cisterns. Immediately south of the base of the two towers, a small frame building housing manual pumps was built. One of the pumps was connected to a well point buried a few feet deep in the water-table aquifer, which was saline, brackish water due to its proximity to tidal waters. Water from here was pumped up to the west tank. The other pump was connected to the potable water cisterns by means of a series of pipes and valves. The cistern having the most water was selected as the current source, and its water was manually-forced up to the tank. The elevated water then provided gravity-fed, pressurized water to the quarters on demand.

The brackish well point water supplied the toilets, and the covered tank furnished water to the other bathroom and kitchen fixtures. Wastewater lines were provided for the toilets only. These drained into a 4-inch terra cotta sewer pipe, which emptied into a single septic tank and drain-field system, buried out on the Gulf beach. After 1944 each quarters would have its own replacement buried septic tank and drain field system. In the case of Quarters 1 and 2 these were situated immediately north of each building. The septic tank of Quarters 3 was located immediately west of its connected building. Effluent from a laundry tub, next to the old privy closet and from the bathtub and sinks also flowed into piping, but these pipes simply led into the ground. The "gray water" simply drained away and was absorbed into the porous seashell based soil.

The Rural Electrification Act of 1936 funded electric service to rural areas throughout the nation. The Lee County Electric Cooperative, which furnishes electric power to our barrier islands, was organized soon after. In 1941, their electric power distribution lines reached Sanibel, Captiva, and Marco islands. However, electric power on the islands was unreliable and subject to long-lasting outages, especially following hurricanes. Therefore, the Coast Guard continued to operate the Sanibel light lantern on acetylene gas. The hand-force pumps in the light station's pump house were soon replaced with electric pumps. Along with a wooden poultry house near Quarters 1, this frame building was subsequently demolished by a hurricane. By late 1958, the pumps for filling the gravity tanks were relocated to the eastern porch of Quarters 1. Only one pump, that which pumped the brackish water for the toilets, was still operable when I arrived to take up residence at the Light Station.

I was delegated the responsibility to regularly climb the toilet water tank, inspect the fluid level, and then operate the pump to keep the tank topped off. I soon rigged up a float inside the tank and connected it to a gauge device I had made and nailed to the outside. A float inside the tank connected to an external counterweight that transferred the water level to a corresponding marked capacity gage

My family at the lighthouse, in 1966. (L-R)—Chuck, Leslie, Jean, and Charles LeBuff. Leslie and Chuck were born in Naples, Florida. Jean was born in Bonita Springs, Florida, and her family's roots go deep in the region. As a teenager her father, Duke Williams, worked on the Punta Rassa cattle docks in 1917 and 1918. Her uncle, Cody Williams, supervised the wild cotton eradication efforts of the U.S. Department of Agriculture on Sanibel and other nearby barrier islands in the late 1930s and 1940s. The agency was trying to eliminate the pink bollworm.

The brown steel tank behind us replaced the cypress cistern after the 1944 hurricane. After the Coast Guard installed their artesian well we piped some of its sulfur water into this rusty tank and then pumped it up to one of the elevated tanks for gravity feed to the quarters. The towers that supported the cypress tanks are visible in the background. An island-wide water system was created in 1965 and the lines reached the lighthouse the year this photo was taken. We used the water in this tank for everything but drinking, until 1966. *From the author's collection* on the outside. This way I could check the water level from ground level and avoided climbing the tower so often. Years earlier, in 1944, a major hurricane had destroyed the ground-level water tank between the structures and took out the elevated wooden cistern of Quarters 2 as well as the station's septic tank and drain field. The Coast Guard quickly replaced both cisterns with steel tanks and installed new septic systems as described above.

Then a 1947 hurricane washed away the metal tank serving Quarters 2 and the Gulf-side staircases of both structures. The stairs, and this particular cistern, were never replaced. With reduced storage capacity, the Coast Guard had to transport more water to the station by tender. The Coast Guard also provided the Light Station crew with a 300-gallon water cart/trailer. When water became low in the cisterns, station personnel would occasionally pull this behind their Jeep to Jake Stokes's residence (this was located just north of Periwinkle Way and a few hundred yards west of Dixie Beach Boulevard). Jake had a high-quality artesian well that was relatively salt-free and he often shared his water with fellow islanders when necessary. The water cart had a pump, and Bob England and the Light Station staff would top off the cisterns at the lighthouse if their supply ran low during the dry season or before a tender was scheduled to arrive. At the time, this water cart was also the only piece of mobile fire-fighting equipment available to the residents of Sanibel Island.

In January 1959, those of us living at Sanibel light had the option of using water from a shallow well for drinking water and general domestic use. This well was a considerable distance inland from the other well-point where the salty, dark toilet water supply originated. It was adequate—once we became used to it. A jet pump with a pressure storage tank supplied water to all three of the quarters, but at times because of demand, the pressure could be very low.

~ ~ ~

IN THE LATE SUMMER OF 1962 we learned that our days at the

lighthouse were possibly numbered. Two visiting engineers from the Seventh Coast Guard District headquarters in Miami brought along some impressive plans they had developed. The district planned to eventually turn the lighthouse property into a fully operational Coast Guard station, including quarters for officers, enlisted men, and dependents; recreational facilities; offices; communication and fueling systems; and some breakwaters and boat docks on the bayside. In time, they expected to base a 95-foot cutter, a number of smaller boats, and a helicopter on their Point Ybel property. They contracted with Miller Brothers, a well-drilling company in Fort Myers, to drill a deep well about 200 feet west of the light tower. If the water met their specifications, they would begin construction of a water system first, after their legal staff worked out some final details with the Lee County Board of County Commissioners, at the county seat in Fort Myers. The plans included a fence, with a guarded gate, across Point Ybel to prohibit public entry.

The Coast Guard's well went ahead on schedule. It was a 6-inch well that was drilled to a total depth of 475 feet, down to the lower Hawthorn aquifer. To prevent contamination of the well's water source or other sources if the quality of the water was good (or bad), 335 feet of 6-inch steel well casing was installed. When completed, the well's artesian head was under greater pressure than any other flowing well that had been drilled before on Sanibel Island, and there had been scores of them. Water from the artesian pressure reached an altitude of over 33 feet above mean sea level, or 28 feet above the ground's elevation at the well site

The capped Coast Guard artesian well near the Sanibel Lighthouse as it appeared in 2007, painted in camouflage tones to help hide it and protect it from vandalism. In 2017 it is difficult to see because of the recovery of conealing vegetation. *Charles LeBuff*

Unfortunately, or fortunately depending on your point of view, the well's water turned out to be less fresh than the Coast Guard's engineers had hoped for. The salinity was a little greater than 1,550 milligrams per liter (mg/l) of dissolved chlorides. The high salt content of the well was a major obstacle to the planned development. Desalinization of such water was possible, but the technology at the time to produce potable water from such highly saline water was ultra-expensive and far beyond the budget appropriated to build a new station. So, it was two strikes against the Coast Guard base. The third strike came in 1962 when the U.S. Coast Guard requested that the Lee County Board of County Commissioners allow its people and their dependents to cross the soon to open new causeway toll-free, but the board turned them down. The plans of a Sanibel Island base by the Coast Guard were scuttled. They changed their planning and went on to build a search and rescue station on the shore of Matanzas Pass, next to Estero Island (Fort Myers Beach).

Those of us residing at the Sanibel Island Light Station breathed a sigh of relief. At the time, I was elated. A salty well and the uncooperative County Commissioners stopped the U.S. Coast Guard and saved Point Ybel. Generations of Sanibel residents and visitors will continue to enjoy its beach, its open spaces, and its historical significance (so I hoped). Although slightly salty to the taste, the Coast Guard's well had value for the Fish and Wildlife Service.

The abandoned well had been fitted with a large shutoff valve so it would not be free-flowing. We bought a roll of several hundred feet of black 1-inch plastic pipe, assorted clamps, and fittings and connected the pipe to the wellhead. I dug a shallow ditch, from the edge of the light station's cleared compound, over to the concrete cistern of Quarters 3 and another to the metal tank between the quarters, and laid the pipe. I elbowed the pipe up and let it discharge, under its own pressure, into the cistern and tank. When these were full, I walked over to the well's valve and shut off the flow.

Most of the LeBuff family inside the lantern room atop the Sanibel light tower, December 1998. L-R, Amber Young; the author, Charles LeBuff; Chuck LeBuff; and Leslie (LeBuff) Young. The Coast Guard graciously opened the light tower for my family and the media, coincidental with the release of my book, *Sanybel Light*. The lens pictured is a 190 mm optic—similar to a modern airport beacon light. It replaced the third optic, the lightship lens discussed earlier, circa 1984. The third lens was installed in 1962, when the illumination source was switched from acetylene to electric. It is currently on display at the Sanibel Historical Village and Museum. *David Meardon*

Once the water was exposed to the air, it's rotten-egg, sulfur water odor dissipated. And, the aerated water really wasn't too offensively salty for the uses we had in mind. By turning a series of valves closing off the intake line to the well-point, we could then distribute the artesian well water from the cistern through the lines and into the plumbing system of all quarters.

During an earlier improvement, we had tied a 1/2-inch metal line into the cistern pipe of Quarters 1 and ran it between the buildings into my kitchen. This gravity-fed line connected drinking water directly into Quarters 2. This meant I no longer had to manhandle heavy 5-gallon glass jugs up and down the stairs; down Tommy Wood's stairs, across the compound, and up my stairs.

In 1965, a group of Sanibel and Captiva residents formed the Island Water Association, Inc. (IWA). Their aim was to operate a water supply and distribution system on the islands. At first they purchased water from an association on nearby Pine Island. This water reached Sanibel through a 10-inch, 9,500-foot-long pipe that ran on the bottom of Pine Island Sound from St. James City on Pine Island to Woodring Point on Sanibel. By 1973, IWA had constructed their own electrodialysis water treatment plant, and by 1975, the capacity of this plant had grown to 2,100,000 gallons a day. In 1980, a Sanibel-based reverse osmosis plant went on-line, and water is no longer purchased from the Greater Pine Island Water Association. The obsolete electrodialysis plant was shut down, and the reverse osmosis plant's current capacity is 4,800,000 gallons a day.

In 1966, the new water system's distribution lines reached the boundary of the lighthouse reservation, and the Fish and Wildlife Service connected up. It took 1,300 feet of 2-inch plastic pipe to get us on-line. All at once, we no longer had to rely on heaven-sent drinking water.

Wildlife at Point Ybel was surprisingly diverse in the years before and until shortly after completion of the first causeway. Beach-nesting birds had both resting and nesting habitat in the days before the recreational area became over-inundated with foolish sun-worshiping beachgoers who are intent only on increasing their risk for future melanomas and other skin disorders. Before that, most public use was done in the early morning when low tide activated shellers to slowly stroll the beach, bowing as they exhibited the famous "Sanibel Stoop." They hoped to discover elusive seashells like junonias, lion's paws, and lady's ears. My own biological interests were always aligned toward the herpetofauna of Sanibel—the amphibians and reptiles, with emphasis on alligators, and later my full-time concentration on loggerhead sea turtles. For anyone having the same or similar interest: I encourage you obtain a copy of my 2014 book, *Amphibians and Reptiles of Sanibel and Captiva Islands, Florida* which I co-authored with Chris Lechowicz of the Sanibel Captiva Conservation Foundation.

The LeBuff family at the lighthouse in December 1998. L-R, Charles LeBuff; Amber Young; Jean LeBuff; Leslie (LeBuff) Young; and Chuck LeBuff. *David Meardon*

Today, a central road bisects the length of the lighthouse reservation. This is shown on a later image. It was completed in the early 1950s and is still used today as an alternate foot access to the lighthouse compound. It is closed to unofficial motor vehicles. This road has borrow ditches on both sides and not long after it was finished a variety of freshwater turtles discovered it. Soon after that, a few American alligators took up residence in the ditches. One of them is suspected to have caught and eaten one of my favorite male miniature poodles, "Sue" (like in the Johnny Cash tune, "A Boy Named Sue")—but I don't dislike or fear alligators. My dog did not have part of an ear missing, but I did keep the fur trimmed shorter on one ear than on the other to maintain Sue's reputation. The canals were re-excavated in the late 1960s to provide better biological mosquito control. Originally a footpath meandered through this area of Point Ybel from the lighthouse Gulf side parking lot to the fishing pier. About equidistant, between the parking lots, the Fish and Wildlife Service constructed a very elaborate comfort station and a sewer treatment plant to the tune of $95,000.00, in 1972 U.S. dollars. This was an aesthetically pleasing primitive-appearing nature trail that wandered through a buttonwood strand that was thickly vegetated with mature buttonwood. Originally, this trail was created with care by Sanibel-Captiva Boy Scout Troop 88, when I was their Scoutmaster. However, not long after the City of Sanibel took over control of Point Ybel they decided to elevate this trail with a boardwalk and in the process they cut down many of the gnarled, ancient-looking buttonwoods. On a positive note, they did remove the exotic and noxious Brazilian pepper that had invaded Point Ybel. The elevated boardwalk of today is a weak example of a nature trail.

The higher elevations of the property, on the low Gulf-front and lower bay-front ridges, supported a small but vigorous population of gopher tortoises and Florida box turtles sometimes nonchalantly wandering over the property. Eastern diamond-backed rattlesnakes that had probably crossed San Carlos Bay with the help of tide and the Caloosahatchee discharge current were commonly found on the upland of Point Ybel and even on the beach there many times.

The beautiful eastern indigo snake, now nationally recognized as a Threatened Species, has been recently extirpated on Sanibel Island. This handsome harmless snake was once abundant on the lighthouse reservation property and most similar habitats on the island.

During spring migration Point Ybel is a great place for birdwatchers to converge. The trail/boardwalk that meanders between Gulf and bay, and the central road, can provide outstanding birding opportunities, especially in the spring, when a variety of migratory warblers stop to rest and nourish themselves after crossing the Gulf of Mexico, or after spanning the Caribbean, on their way back north for the summer.

Another natural asset we enjoyed during our lighthouse tenure was the often outstanding shelling that was available at our doorstep. Our children thrived on the beach and each picked up some high quality specimen seashells. Some of them are still part of our family collection. Personally, I found five junonias on the Point Ybel beach over the years, but I consider none of them in any way perfect.

My three-year-old son, Chuck, is pictured holding one of the large eastern indigo snakes that lived near our lighthouse home in 1964. Habitat destruction because of real estate development, road kills, alteration of habitat due to the invasion of exotic noxious plants, and over-collecting for the pet trade eventually resulted in the demise of this handsome, ecologically valuable snake on the island. There has been no valid, documented evidence of this species on Sanibel Island in recent years.

When I wrote my historical novel, *The Calusan*, memories of Chuck and his interaction with this particular snake helped me develop a child character named Logan Clark. In my book Logan is the son of Ivy Clark, a fictional assistant lighthouse keeper at the Sanibel Lighthouse.

The Sanibel light tower was Chuck's "jungle gym." He was once "busted" after he had shimmied to an elevation just under the lower gallery in the top of the tower—he had climbed all the way up—on the outside! *George Weymouth*

CHAPTER 6

A parade of lighthouse photos and postcards . . .

OVER TIME, TENS OF THOUSANDS OF PHOTOGRAPHS have been taken of the Sanibel Lighthouse. They were never assembled in a cohesive presentation to track the physical changes to the Sanibel Island Light Station over the last 100-plus years, until Deb Gleason and I put together our book, *Sanibel and Captiva Islands*. This book was published by Arcadia Publishing as part of their Postcard History Series. In this chapter I will do that, and more, again. The photos that best interpret the evolution of the Sanibel Island Light Station through the years are postcards. I have selected a few, many produced by the Sanibel Packing Company (Bailey's General Store), for this review and include captions that fully discuss their timeline and condition.

This circa 1885 photograph is one of the earliest available of the Sanibel Island Light Station. This view is looking southerly from the bayside. The existing brick oil house has not yet been constructed, nor have the small screen porches been built. The access stairways are visible, as are colonial-style window shutters. The lantern room is shrouded with its daytime curtains to protect the nighttime-revolving Fresnel optic from the intense heat that its series of parallel lenses may generate when they are exposed to the high temperatures of direct sunlight radiation. Overheated prisms could crack and they were extremely expensive to replace. Some light keepers also feared that an optic's magnified sunlight could focus enough on the ground below to start fires that would quickly threaten their facility. *From the Internet*

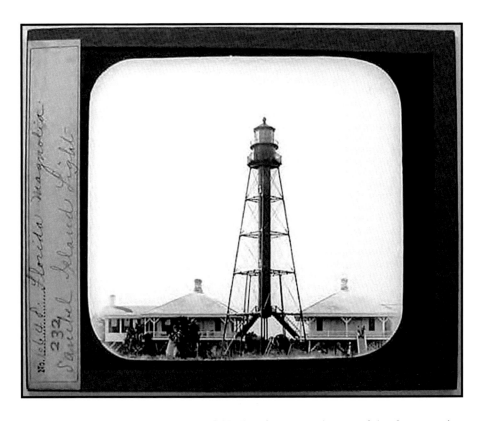

A lantern slide, also from about 1885. The figures at the top of the Quarters 1 stairway are most likely the first light keeper Dudley Richardson and his wife. This image was later adapted for use on a cigarette card from the period. (See below). *Public domain*

Sanibel Island Light—One of a series of 50 different cards featuring American lighthouses, produced by Hassan Cork Tip Cigarettes in 1911. *From the author's collection*

This photo of the Light Station is from the bay, circa 1908. Two boathouses are visible; one in the foreground over the water and another onshore. Note the well-vegetated woods to the east of the station (left of boathouses). In 1923, when the Sanibel Island Lighthouse Reservation was downsized to its present boundary it contained about 54 acres of land. Today (2017), it contains about 23 acres of land—the rest, once to the east and south has washed away and erosion of Point Ybel continues. *Islander Trading Post*

The Light Station from the garden-like Gulf side, circa 1920. Pathways lead to the beach and chicken coops. The small cubicle building is a pump house. A new water distribution system and quarters remodeling and modernizing would be in place by 1923. A major hurricane in 1926 would later change the station's appearance. Distribution of electricity would not cross the bay and serve Sanibel and Captiva islands until 1941. *Sanibel Packing Company*

The Sanibel Island Light Station, circa 1933. The stationary third-order Fresnel optic that was in place from 1923 until 1962 is visible, as is the cistern of Quarters 2. The small building in the foreground is a chicken coop. The single rail perimeter fence delineates the well-manicured, vegetation-free compound. Vegetation outside the compound is maintained low, for visibility, cooling airflow, wind-control of biting insects, and most importantly for fire control. This is a Sanibel Packing Company card. *Islander Trading Post*

A hand-colored 1935 post card, photographed from the beach and looking eastward at the lighthouse. Since Hurricane Charley, in August 2004, the light tower is again very visible and has regained its prominent landmark status, from whichever point of the compass one can approach Sanibel Island. *Islander Trading Post*

The Sanibel Lighthouse in 1948. A series of major hurricanes in the 1940s had severely damaged the station's facilities. Storm-caused erosion had undermined Quarters 2, and its cistern was swept away. With consideration of future damaging weather events in mind, the U.S. Coast Guard automated the light and withdrew their personnel, in 1949. In this image the lighthouse is being repainted and this is noticeable by the shinier appearance of the upper section. *Islander Trading Post*

A 1958 aerial view of the Light Station. The compound is clearly discernible, as are all structures and the advanced erosion. The newly constructed center road that was mentioned earlier is visible to the upper left. The white building to the far right is the last of the station's boathouses—it was torn down in 1961. This is the condition and configuration of the station when my family and I became residents. The Coast Guard pier that was in place in 1958 was located to the right of the boathouse. *From the author's collection*

The light tower and Quarters 1, in 1965. At the time, this surviving cistern served both quarters—the brick base continues to stand in 2017. The tank survived until it had dried out enough for the wood to shrink and it collapsed a decade after this photograph was taken. Note the ladder on the roof above the cistern. I had placed it there because within a day or two after the photographer happened to take this shot I would don boots and climb down inside the drained cistern tank to give it its annual cleaning—once we were sure rainy season had started and we could depend on it refilling quickly. *Isander Trading Post*

Circa 1977, during franchise negotiations, Palmer Cabelvision (forerunner to Comcast on Sanibel and Captiva islands) presented each member of the Sanibel City Council with a watercolor print of the Sanibel Lighthouse. I asked for a second print and made frames from the old clear-heart cypress lumber from the Quarters 1 cistern for each of my children. The original artwork was created by famed watercolor artist Paul N. Norton (1909-1984). *Charles LeBuff.*

The light tower and compound in 1967. Note the metal tank on the ground and the water storage towers between the quarters. Also quite visible are the original wood frame double-hung windows that provided light into the stairway tube. During the 2013 maintenance of the Sanibel light tower the restoration was not accomplished to attain the structure's basic originality of color. Among other elements, the City of Sanibel failed to replace the existing windows with windows that matched the original design. *Charles LeBuff*

The light tower and quarters with the elevated water tanks between them, in 1959. My family and I lived in Quarters 2 (right) at this time. It was during the worst of the erosion. On some extra-high spring tides I occasionally could throw a cast net off the far end of the porch and catch striped mullet. A few times friends and I cast into the surf from the porch with plugs known as MirrOlures® and caught sizeable snook. The beach began to accrete and naturally started to restore itself by 1970. Note the beach-invading Australian pine saplings in the foreground. *From the author's collection*

Quarters 2 in 1959. Erosion is nearing its worst in living memory. Note the condition of the clapboard siding. This was later covered by asbestos shingle siding to match what had been done to Quarters 1 in 1952. This photo was taken many years before I enclosed the right-hand end of the porch to add storage/office space. It would have been a good day to try for snook from the porch. *Charles LeBuff*

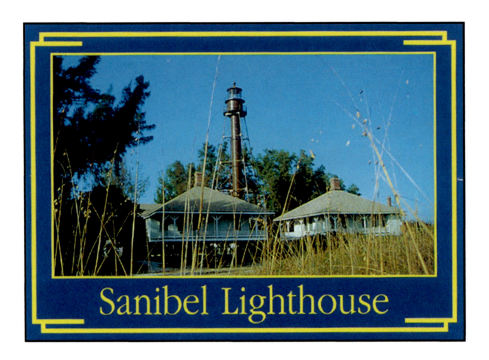

Sanibel Lighthouse

The Light Station, 1993. This photograph was taken before Hurricane Charley (2004). This Category 4 hurricane tore up the Lee and Charlotte County barrier islands and the mainland for a considerable distance inland. The powerful winds blew down most of the trees in this photo. The tall Australian pines (*Casuarina*) pictured standing beyond the quarters can all trace their lineage to the trees planted by Sanibel's U.S. Lighthouse Service personnel in the 1930s. At least two species of these trees were introduced to the island by some of the Bailey family and other farmers in the early 1920s. Their removal, by either man or powerful forces of nature, is an environmental plus. People who profess to favor the continued existence of these trees on barrier islands—they are commonly known as "Australian pine 'huggers'"—seem to lack environmental astuteness, and in my book, (This is my book!) I grant them no credibility whenever they speak about the fictitious virtues of this undesirable introduced exotic tree. I could speak volumes on the detrimental effect they have on the island's ecology, particularly negative impacts they have on sea turtle nesting on the barrier islands of South Florida. *Gerri Much*

Chapter 7
In the end . . .

WHAT DOES THE FUTURE HOLD FOR THE SANIBEL Island Light Station? After the publication of my book *Sanybel Light* I was invited to serve on the board of directors of the Florida Lighthouse Association. This organization was founded in 1996. Its stated mission *"is to safeguard Florida's remaining lighthouses for future generations by supporting community based restoration, preservation, and education efforts."* I represented the Sanibel Lighthouse on the association's board for several years. While serving I found myself in a difficult situation since I had no official connection to the city government, or to the Sanibel Historical Society, or for that matter to the Light Station. Finding I could not effectively represent the Sanibel Island Light Station I opted to no longer serve the organization. As far as I know, as of this writing now many years later, no one has yet been appointed to replace me as the representative of the Sanibel Lighthouse on the group's board.

Over the years since my unofficial connection ended, I have been concerned over issues that are related to the structural stability of the light tower, rehabilitation of the historic station compound, and proper interpretation of this historic site.

In March, 2007, I launched the short-lived online *Southwest Florida Natural History Newsletter*. In the June issue I featured an article that discussed my view of what I considered at the time to be the deplorable condition of the Sanibel Island Light Station. I called for the restoration of the Light Station compound and full historical interpretation of the site's relationship to the history of Sanibel Island and the immediate region. Two newspapers covered my concerns and in response to one of the articles I outlined a draft for a four-point plan to accomplish what I consider to be minimal requirements for an ongoing program which will result in the proper restoration and long-overdue historical interpretation of the facility. These straightforward suggestions apparently fell on deaf ears at all responsible levels of the city government. There were no public responses whatsoever from anyone connected to the Sanibel Historical Society or from any official connected to the City of Sanibel at the time. This plan has been modified because at this writing city employees are no longer residing in the quarters. My suggested plan for the Sanibel Lighthouse follows:

1. Sanibel's Historical Preservation Committee should begin work to restore Quarters 1 to an earlier condition. I would pick 1923, because actual remodeling drawings are available for that year. After renovation, Quarters 1 would transition into a Visitor Center/Museum with a modest entrance fee. These funds would be pledged to funding educational interpretation and maintenance at the Light Station. Required work at this stage would include replacing brick and re-pointing the mortar joints of the cistern base and the oil house, replacing the wooden cistern at Quarters 1 with one duplicating the original, and re-roofing the oil house with corrugated metal. Reinstallation of the former screen porches and stairways from each quarter's deck to the light tower landing should be seriously considered. In the future, budgets should include cost of having the asbestos shingle siding removed in stages and the original wooden siding hidden beneath it sandblasted and painted with modern paints. The iron pilings, which support both quarters, should be assessed for their structural integrity. I suggest the city procure *exact duplicates* of these pilings, but rather than metal have the replacements manufactured from pre-stressed concrete. The original

metal supports would then be replaced systematically: scheduled over time, and painted to match the original color (I'm sure they were not white! The present color was curiously selected by someone associated with the City of Sanibel). It seems that many of the existing supports may have reached their maximum life expectancy—they are, after all, 133 years old at this writing. Lighthouse artifacts now housed at the Historical Village and Museum would move to the Quarters 1 museum.

2. Engineers from the Sanibel Public Works Department should survey and stake the extremities of the historic lighthouse compound plus add an additional predetermined distance beyond the perimeter of that survey. A public works crew would then move in and remove every piece of vegetation that is now growing inside the compound. Any candidate plants worthy of relocation would be transplanted to the outside of the clearing. At this time all the existing chain-link fencing and other fencing would be removed. Remove, or relocate elsewhere to the outside the compound, the garage at Quarters 2 (I built this in 1976). Grade the entire compound site down to the grade of its original construction level (1884). This would expose the pads (the concrete encasing them should be removed) of the light tower for periodic maintenance. Install a well-aligned new chain link security fence and appropriate gates around the site, just outside a replica of the compound's 1923 boundary's single-rail, decorative fence that is erected after clearing and grading. The compound's ground surface would then continue to be managed as a vegetation-free zone. That is, with the exception of coconut palms.

3. The city or historical society should hire a Sanibel Island Light Station Curator/Caretaker and offer Quarters 2 as a residence for that employee and his or her family. Then the complex restoration of the exterior of Quarters 2 should begin. This would include tearing out the cubicle of my former office that I described earlier. It negatively impacts the structure's integrity. When financing becomes available to continue restoration, a replica cistern and base should be built in the proper location and period-style gutters should be installed along with faux downspouts on both quarters.

Time will have to judge what happens to the Sanibel Island Light Station. When I first raised the issues about the station's poor condition, the leadership of the City of Sanibel took no positive action that indicated any serious effort was being made on their part to halt the trend of neglect.

The city's excuses for their inaction ranged from self-inflicted budget deficits, lack of ownership of the property, and potential environmental cleanup issues. In my opinion the City of Sanibel had no genuine excuse for their inaction. Why didn't they expeditiously push our district congressman to seek an appropriation for any environmental cleanup required at the lighthouse, if one was actually needed? Our congressional representative could have used his office to light a fire under the Bureau of Land Management to get them moving and complete a transfer or sale of the property to the city much earlier.

Everything changed in 2010. The land and structures of the Sanibel Island Light Station were sold to the City of Sanibel by the U.S. Bureau of Land Management for the ridiculous sum of $447.70. Yes, you read that correctly . . . *$447.70!* Did the federal government cut the City of Sanibel a break, or did the city "buy a pig in a poke"?

The integrity of the Light Station is now solidly under the purview of the city and at this time they are fully responsible for its future maintenance. The first financial impact under this obligation occurred in mid-2013 when the city contracted to have the light tower repaired and repainted. A contractor, the low bidder among 11 who submitted bids, agreed to do the work outlined in the invitation-to-bid for the sum of $269,563. Work began in mid-June 2013 with a tentative completion in September. The city had expected to pay about $300,000 for the work, so the project came in under budget. A historic preservation grant of $50,000 from the Florida Division of Historical Resources further reduced the city's capital outlay.

Remember, this is not a one-time cost. A comparable sum of money will be expended every 10 or 12 years; just for the light tower's scheduled maintenance. Maintenance of the tower and the keeper's quarters and erosion control on Point Ybel will amount to a significant sum over the years. In 2013 I wrote: *Watch for beach parking fees to increase on Sanibel Island.* They have since and they will again.

The Sanibel City Council made another positive step when members voted to allow the Sanibel Historical Museum and Village to become independent from direct city control. The Sanibel Historical Museum and Village, Inc., complex is now operated as a not-for-profit organization (501[c] [3]). I extend congratulations to the efforts of the late historical committee chairman, Sam Bailey, and the dedicated membership of the Sanibel Historical Preservation Committee which is now chaired by my coauthor (*Sanibel and Captiva Islands*) and long-time Sanibellian, Deborah Gleason. If you care about the future of the Sanibel Island Lighthouse, and its best interests, please assist this new organization financially—become a member! I truly hope that it will be a short transition period for the nonprofit entity to mature, spread its wings, and successfully negotiate and get control of the management of the Sanibel Island Light Station. Led by their history, the people of Sanibel Island may yet do those light keepers of old proud.

Each new dawn brings renewed hope for the restoration of Sanibel Island's long-neglected landmark, the traditional former U.S. Lighthouse Service and U.S. Coast Guard compound on Point Ybel. The day has come for improved protection and preservation of its historic structural assets and the professional development of an educational interpretive program that is designed especially for the Sanibel Island Light Station, to educate the thousands of visitors who are attracted to its historic grounds. *Gary Cole*

Suggested Further Reading

Sanybel Light, A Historical Autobiography—A Wildlife Life on a Florida Barrier Island by Charles LeBuff—A comprehensive history of Sanibel Island, its lighthouse and the National Wildlife Refuge. Both a paperback and an e-Book edition are available.

The Calusan, by Charles LeBuff—A historical adventure novel with a Sanibel Island and Sanibel Lighthouse theme. Both a paperback and an e-Book edition are available.

J. N. "Ding" Darling National Wildlife Refuge, by Charles LeBuff—Published by Arcadia Publishing—A pictorial history of this popular wildlife refuge and available at select island book and gift shops.

Sanibel and Captiva Islands, by Deborah Gleason and Charles LeBuff—Published by Arcadia Publishing—An island history based on vintage postcards and available at select island book and gift shops.

The Sea Shell Islands, by Elinore Dormer—A history of Sanibel and Captiva—available at the Sanibel Historical Village and select island bookshops.

Sanibel's Story: Voices and Images from Calusa to Incorporation, by Betty Anholt—A pictorial book covering the complete history of the island. Available at island bookshops and the Sanibel Historical Museum and Village gift shop.

The Nature of Things on Sanibel, by George Campbell—Currently out-of-print, but copies become available from time to time in the used book trade.

The Other Side of the Bridge, by Ted Levering—A fact-based, delightful novel—Currently out-of-print but still available online.

Florida Lighthouse Trail, edited by Thomas Taylor—Published by the Florida Lighthouse Association and available through their website or island bookshops.

A Brief History of Sanibel Island, by Marya Repko—Published by ECity Publishing. A concise illustrated history of Sanibel Island and available wherever books are sold on the islands.

Historic Sanibel and Captiva Islands: Tales of Paradise by Jeri Magg—An island history that spans 300 years. This title is available at select island book and gift shops.

Living Sanibel: A Nature Guide to Sanibel & Captiva Islands, by Charles Sobczak. This title is available at island book and gift shops.

When you are visiting Sanibel and Captiva islands don't forget to save time for a stop at the Sanibel Historical Museum and Village. It is located on Dunlop Road, near the Sanibel Public Library and Sanibel City Hall. I assume that it goes without saying that you'll also visit the Sanibel Island Light Station. If you agree with me, that the Light Station compound and structures need serious rehabilitation to their original appearance, please make an effort to telephone or visit the Sanibel Parks and Recreation Department and convey your concerns.

The Captiva Historical Society has enlarged their facility at the Captiva Community House. Visitors will find their historical displays enjoyable and a walkthrough of the adjacent Captiva Cemetery interesting.

APPENDUM*

Locally-made Movies You May Find Interesting

Parts of some of the following motion pictures were filmed on Sanibel or Captiva islands and others on nearby islands, you'll find them on DVD if marked (*), and available through Warner Brothers Create on Demand if marked (**).

Distant Drums— 1951, starring Gary Cooper.

Wind Across the Everglades**—1958, Starring Burl Ives.

Night Moves*—1975, starring Gene Hackman and Melanie Griffith.

Blue Sky*—1994, starring Jessica Lange and Tommy Lee Jones.

Captiva Island*1995, starring Ernest Borgnine and Arte Johnson.

~ ~ ~

* Included just for the fun of it.

Charles LeBuff—*Photo by Deb Gleason.*

A Note About the Author

CHARLES LeBUFF WAS BORN IN MASSACHUSETTS and his family moved to Bonita Springs, Florida, in 1952. He began a long federal career with the U.S. Fish and Wildlife Service in 1957 at their Red Tide Field Investigation Laboratory in Naples. Then, in 1958, he was selected to fill the number two position at the Sanibel National Wildlife Refuge on Sanibel Island, Florida. He spent thirty-two years as a Wildlife Technician at this refuge; renamed J. N. "Ding" Darling National Wildlife Refuge in 1967. Charles retired from his position in 1990, but remained on the island until 2005.

During his time on Sanibel Island, and in other than his official work capacity, he served as president of the Sanibel-Captiva Audubon Society, was a founding board member of the Sanibel-Captiva Conservation Foundation, was twice elected to the Sanibel City Council, serving his community from 1974 to 1980, and he founded and directed the loggerhead turtle conservation project, Caretta Research, Inc.

Today, he and his wife Jean, live near Fort Myers, Florida, where he lectures, writes, carves wood, pursues an ongoing interest in wildlife photography, flies his Phantom 4 drone, and is learning to master the acoustic guitar.

Made in the USA
Lexington, KY
14 November 2017